# THE NEW INTIMACY

## Open-Ended Marriage and Alternative Lifestyles

## by Ronald Mazur

toExcel

San Jose   New York   Lincoln   Shanghai

**The New Intimacy**
Open-Ended Marriage and Alternative Lifestyles

This edition published by toExcel Press,
an imprint of iUniverse.com, Inc.

For information address:
iUniverse.com, Inc.
620 North 48th Street
Suite 201
Lincoln, NE 68504-3467
www.iuniverse.com

ISBN  0-595-00102-5

*DEDICATED WITH LOVE*

*to friends*
*who've shared with us*
*joys and elations,*
*sorrows and aggravations.*
*And*
*to persons everywhere*
*who deeply care,*
*who are aware,*
*and seek to share*
*intimacy.*

# PREFACE FOR THE 21ST CENTURY

The close of the 20th century has witnessed the minority status of the traditional family in America. As of 1998, only 26 percent of households were married couples with children according to the National Opinion Research Center of the University of Chicago. In contrast, households with unmarried adults with no children rose to 32 percent, more than double the rate in the 1972 survey from the same source. Clearly, family relationships have changed in this society. Alternative lifestyles are no longer on the fringe.

Intimate relationships in the 21st century are more complex than in the early 1970s. For instance, the explosion of the HIV/AIDS terror in the 1980s caused temporary fear of sexual encounters. Condoms were elevated to essential equipment, at least in politically correct gay and heterosexual coupling. And enormous public relations exposure was given to options for maintaining sexual abstinence. While there are valid reasons for the use of condoms and for the delay or avoidance of sexual intercourse, it seemed as if these behaviors were the only permissible ones. Gender struggles were exacerbated and intimacy issues were confusing. There was considerable backlash against healthy sexuality education, while advances were made in the scare tactics of repressive sex propaganda. The irony is that people grounded in forthright sexuality education have so many more pleasurable options than only sexual intercourse.

From 1972 through 1989, I worked as a health educator for the University Health Services of the University of Massachusetts at Amherst. As director of the Peer Sexuality Education Program, and also from 1985-1989 the AIDS Education Coordinator for the University, I experienced the impact of those stressful events. There was no confidence that HIV/AIDS, and whatever forthcoming micro-organisms will yet attack us, could be defeated.

On the threshold of a new millennium, now is an opportune and urgent time to give voice to the intimacies of alternative lifestyles, including open marriage. As complex as the issues may be, the many people who choose non-traditional living arrangements deserve a new vocabulary to explore for themselves. It is not enough, for example, for those without children to be referred to as "empty nesters: or "childless" if they are pleased to be child-free. Traditional monogamy is still the prize for countless adults searching for meaning and love in their lives. That search is honored by myriad religious and societal supports. It is to non-traditionalists, to those ready for new life and love affirmations, that this book is offered with joy. The evolution of human consciousness prepares the way for the unfolding of our universal polyamorous potential. Let the pioneers be unafraid to move beyond the ancient limits of relationships to the new intimacy of responsible erotic freedom. May the new millennium be the end of pleasure-phobia.

It is a great pleasure to know that we can keep a dialogue going electronically. My e-mail address is ronmazur@eroticspirituality.com/. I can respond to your delights and concerns as well as keep you informed on the progress of our website community. Let me hear from you!

—Ron Mazur

# CONTENTS

# AFFIRMATIONS AND ACKNOWLEDGMENTS

I wrote these words, but share the creation of their substance and significance with Joyce Mazur. Indeed, the essence of this book is our co-creation of open-ended marriage with supportive intimate relationships. Though the scribe and verbal architect is designated author, in truth, this volume reflects the dimensions of many sharers, planners, and dreamers. Its publication is an act of affirmation between Joyce and me, and thus the plural mode of the Dedication. The writing of this work has been difficult, and the living of it has been arduous; may the former be as helpful to others as the latter has been vibrantly enriching to us.

The encouragement, inspiration, and/or criticism of particular colleague-friends is also joyfully acknowledged. Without benefit of professional titles or positions, they are: deryck calderwood, Joan Constantine, Larry Constantine, Barbara Hollerorth, Holly Hollerorth, Lester Kirkendall, Roger Libby, Tom Maurer, Lonny Myers, Jeanette Peck, Jessie Potter, Bob Rimmer, Pat Schreiner, Don Shaw, Anne Welbourne, and Thayer Williams.

Let it be stated explicitly, that the above persons do not necessarily agree with the particulars of this book.

A gift of friendship was bestowed by the volunteer typist of the manuscript, Barbara Copelas: a gift all the more cherished since she personally repudiates most of the text.

And finally, an expression of profound gratitude to Ray Bentley, the Beacon Press editor who diligently guided the work to completion.

Ron Mazur
*Amherst, Massachusetts*
*January 29, 1973*

# INTIMATIONS OF INTIMACY

Intimacy
is an exquisite event of Being in touch.

Intimacy
is crying together with shared feelings
of joy or suffering.

Intimacy
is the liquid communion of mutual sucking.

Intimacy
is hate defending dashed dreams
and ruined hopes
yet seeing the other's value
in spite of emotional disasters.

Intimacy
is freedom and commitment in creative tension

Intimacy
is the agony of apology
and the grace of forgiveness.

Intimacy
is acceptance of each other
with humor and warmth
when the masks, postures, and roles
have been stripped away.

Intimacy
is a massage by loving hands.

Intimacy
is what we neglect when we have it
and become desperate for when we lose it.

Intimacy
is a sudden smile and open eyes
which say, "Yes, I know."

Intimacy
is a myriad of delights
which bodies together can share
under the multitudinous
sensual benedictions of Nature

Intimacy
is an exquisite event of Being in touch.

# CHAPTER ONE / OPEN-ENDED MARRIAGE VERSUS ADULTERY

O O O O O O O O O O O O O O O O O O O O O O O O O O O
O O O O O O O O O O O O O O O O O O O O O O O O O O
O O O O O O O O O O O O O O O O O O O O O O O O O O O
O O O O O O O O O O O O O O O O O O O O O O O O O O O
O O O O O O O O O O O O O O O O O O O O O O O O O O O O
O O O O O O O O O O O O O O O O O O O O O O O O O O O
O O O O O O O O O O O O O O O O O O O O O O O O O O O O
O O O O O O O O O O O O O O O O O O O O O O O O O O O
O O O O O O O O O O O O O O O O O O O O O O O O O O O

Is it possible to create a marital relationship which is non-possessive, encourages personal growth, and values sexual liberty? We believe it is not only a possibility, but that thousands of men and women in our society are eager to build open-ended marriages.

There are, of course, people who will consider open-ended marriage to be nothing more than a brazen form of institutionalized adultery. Some will tolerate it as a regrettable yet personal relational preference which is none of their concern. Others will condemn and actively oppose it as a perversion of morals and a destructive influence on monogamous marriage and family life. We realize at the outset that there will be many types of negative criticism of our proposal for a new model of marriage, but we feel that the time is long overdue for a radical reappraisal of the way in which we commit ourselves to each other and relate with interpersonal intimacy.

Our hope is to initiate constructive discussion of a specific form of alternative lifestyle. At the very least, those who move with us through these pages will be able to clarify what it is they really value in the marital relationship and what they hope to achieve in the adventure of creating intimacy

1

with other persons. While sociologists, psychologists, and anthropologists continue to gather and analyze valuable data on individuals, small groups, and larger populations, we wish to begin a more personal kind of dialogue. Sometimes, what scholars chart in professional journals can be more deeply understood by encountering individuals who are willing to speak in an open and more direct manner.

What we have to say in this book is a continued and more comprehensive exploration of a dialogue begun in *Commonsense Sex* (Boston: Beacon Press, 1968). At that time we agonized over the serious decision to suggest in print (chapter nine, "Parents and Lovers") an alternative to conventional monogamy which we referred to as "monogamous nonpromis cuous pluralism." The phrase now sounds hilariously awkward, and it was not until 1970 that the more appropriate term "open-ended marriage" was used in an address presented at the annual meeting of the National Council of Family Relations.[1] It is a term which has since been used by other professionals in the field of family life research and education. In any case, "Chapter Nine" got to be almost a code word. *Commonsense Sex* was written primarily for unmarried young adults as a basis for discussion and reappraisal of sexual behavior and values. Naturally, parents and older adults would respond with more intense interest to a consideration of "Parents and Lovers." Sooner or later, whether we were at professional conferences, conducting sex education workshops, counseling couples, or at a cocktail party, anyone who read the book would say, "Tell us more about chapter nine." That chapter, which considered the meanings of adultery and extramarital intimacy, was addressed to unmarried young adults for three reasons: to help maturing children better understand some of the interpersonal tensions between their parents; be aware of some of the emotional consequences if they became sexually involved with a married person; and prepare them for the realistic possibility of their desire for experiences with intimacy after their own marriage.

Actually, this discussion of adultery and extramarital relations in 1968 was neither radical nor preposterous. Dr. Paul Gebhard, successor to Dr. Alfred Kinsey and director of the Institute for Sex Research has said: "If I were to make an educated guess as to the cumulative incidence figures [of extramarital sexual experience] for 1968, they'd be about 60 percent for males and 35 to 40 percent for females."[2] Although Dr. Gebhard did not consider this a revolution in sex behavior as measured against Kinsey's 1948 and 1953 statistics on male and female sexual behavior, he was nevertheless referring to millions of men and women who participated in unconventional marital behavior. And there is every reason to believe in a continuation of previous trends upward in the numbers of persons who will risk challenging traditional prohibitions against extramarital sexual intimacy.

In America, the 1920's mark the time of the radical questioning of the nature of marriage and man-woman relationships. Although there are certainly literary antecedents, it was Judge Ben B. Lindsey's *The Companionate Marriage*, published in 1927 (with Wainwright Evans as co-author), which provoked widespread and heated debate on the subject. Lindsey was acrimoniously accused of promoting "free love" and "trial marriage," but his own judgment of his proposal as being "conventionally respectable" has been sustained by time. He defined companionate marriage as "legal marriage, with legalized birth control, and with the right to divorce by mutual consent for childless couples, usually without payment of alimony.[3] Judge Lindsey suffered the condemnation of the "respectable" people of that time, but the prophetic nature of his ideas about legalized birth control and the right to divorce by mutual consent for childless couples is now obvious.

More recent writings reflect the new thinking and behavior in regard to marital styles and sexuality. An examination of the books in our personal library leads us to suggest that the decade of the sixties was more progressive than we had realized as we lived through those years. The following nonfiction books, for example, are suggestive of the daring and straightforward re-evaluation of traditional monogamy and fidelity which has been taking place. These books are not of equal social significance, but each in its own way conveys aspects of the quest for that kind of meaningful marriage which allows for sexual variety and multirelational intimacy.

" " " " "

*The Love Elite* by Arthur H. Hirsch (1963)[4]
Based on a study of over 100,000 love letters and thousands of interviews and conversations, the author draws a portrait of a new woman who seeks to realize her emancipation through sexual fulfillment, who is not restrained from this goal by social taboos—"The women of the love elite evaluate sexual behavior on the basis of its quality: its affectionate character, its wholesomeness, and the benefits derived. *They believe that a new age with a new ethic has made acceptable new sources of happiness, of which sexual intimacy in or out of wedlock is one*" (p. 20). Though the author does not grasp the full dimensions of women's liberation (e.g., "It seems a part of nature's plan that woman yearns for the supreme fulfillment: to be made pregnant and to become a mother," p. 255) he nevertheless has thought-provoking chapters on "The Re-evaluation of Virginity" and on "The Re-evaluation of Marital Fidelity."

*Toward a Quaker View of Sex* (1964)[5]
It will astonish those who know about inhibiting and negative factors organized religion brings to the understanding and living of human sexuality to realize that extensive re-evaluations are taking place among religious groups. A case in point is this "essay by a group of Friends" published in England. The first edition was withdrawn from circulation because of bold implications

concerning extramarital intimacy. The revised edition, however, maintains the possibility that such relationships can be constructive. "We recognize," the group maintains, "that while most examples of the 'eternal triangle' are produced by boredom and primitive misconduct, others may arise from the fact that the very experience of loving one person with depth and perception may sensitize a man or a woman to the lovable qualities in others. . . . The man who swallows the words, 'I love you' when he meets another woman, may in that moment and for that reason begin to resent his wife's existence" (p. 45). We are assured that "it is also true that love may be creative if honestly acknowledged though not openly confessed" (p. 45), but in the endeavor to make morality creative and personally responsible, we are also free to determine when we are in a situation which makes extramarital loving enriching and good. We assume also that the wife has the capacity to resent her husband's existence when she is constrained from acknowledging or confessing love for another man.

*The Significant Americans* by John F. Cuber and Peggy B. Harroff (1965)[6]
Subtitled "A Study of Sexual Behavior among the Affluent," this book is based upon extensive interviews over a five-year period with 437 "clearly successful" men and women. "They are among the most highly educated and are the models of achievement to which the ambitious aspire" (p. 5). Cuber and Harroff offer many refreshing observations about the quality of the relationships among this group. Of special pertinence are their conclusions about self-image and guilt. "Such self-directing people—our data suggest a clear majority of them—simply do not develop the overpowering negative emotional residues that they are supposed to, according to the simplitudes of textbooks on mental

hygiene or on how to be happy though married . . . so many calmly acknowledged that they had in fact done, or are now doing, the things which are supposed to lead to psychological disaster (e.g., abortions, premarital promiscuity, or extramarital affairs); yet no such disaster has occurred. Quite the reverse—they remain healthy, creative people whose talents help to give direction to the collective human enterprise" (pp. 177–178). Again, they emphasize the conclusion: "most of them with such experiences expressed no guilt and said they would do exactly the same things if they had the same choice again. We found very little evidence of guilt about unchastity or adultery" (p. 179).

*Honest Sex* by Rustum and Della Roy (1968)[7]

Rustum and Della Roy, both prominent in graduate teaching and research in the physical sciences, are also both actively involved with experiments in Christian Community. Somewhat like the group of Friends who embarked on a joint effort to find a modern sex ethic, the Roys worked with their colleagues of the Sycamore Community of Pennsylvania to present a comprehensive framework for a contemporary Christian ethic of love and human sexuality. It is indeed an honest work, ambitious in scope and alert to new dimensions of loving human relationships. One of their conclusions, relevant to our concern, follows.

"We find that sexual relations with persons other than a spouse are becoming more common. When other criteria of appropriateness are fulfilled, such relations do not necessarily destroy or hurt a marriage, nor do they inflict an unbearable hurt on the partner not involved. Indeed, when human need is paramount, such relationships can serve as the vehicle of faithfulness to God. When deep relationships exist between the persons, we find the danger from such experience not to be prohibitive if the spouse is progressively informed of the development of the relationship and the marriage itself is secure. From an ethical point of view we believe that it is important not to ask the wrong question nor use the wrong words. It is important not to ask whether coitus has occurred; it is important to avoid words such as *adultery*. The important question is: Were relations deepened so as to make all the persons concerned more able to become whole, to give to others, and so on? We foresee an inevitable and rapid increase in such co-marital relationships and regard it as the Church's urgent business to provide guidelines for the most creative conduct within them" (pp. 107–108).

We find the forthrightness and courage of *Honest Sex* to be inspiring.

*Adultery for Adults* by Joyce Peterson and Marilyn Mercer (1968)[8]

Written in a lighthearted, delightful, and sometimes tongue-in-cheek manner, this book offers practical guidelines to "Horizontal Enrichment" through "creative adultery." The authors claim that their book fills the need for official rules for America's most popular sport. Their dos and don'ts range from the helpful to the ridiculous. Perhaps the significance of the book is simply that it was published and distributed in this country, and that it treats the secretive and scandalous subject of adultery like a carefree body-shopping list.

*The Affair* by Morton Hunt (1969)[9]

Morton Hunt is an accomplished journalist who specializes in the study of human relationships. His research method utilized diaries and letters, nearly forty interviews with professionals knowledgeable about the subject, previously published data, 360 completed questionnaires designed and administered by an independent research team, and ninety-one tape-recorded depth interviews which he conducted. He records the actual experiences of men and women involved in this type of behavior, and classifies his material according to the degree of involvement of each participant. Hunt considers the degree of involvement to be the most significant factor related to the meanings and consequences of extramarital affairs. His conclusion is stated in the context of "situation ethics." "The evidence," he believes, "clearly shows that in some circumstances an extramarital affair severely damages the marriage, the participants, and even such innocent bystanders as the children; and in other circumstances it does none of these things, and is of no consequence; and in still other circumstances it benefits the marriage by ameliorating discontent, or shatters the marriage but benefits the individual by awakening him to his own emotional needs and capabilities. I therefore believe that each extramarital act ought to be judged as morally evil, morally neutral, or morally good, according to the totality of the circumstances and the effects on all concerned" (p. xv).

*Extramarital Relations* edited by Gerhard Neubeck (1969)[10]

The editor of this collection of fourteen articles is a former president of the American Association of Marriage Counselors who conducts a postdoctoral program on marriage counseling and maintains a private practice in that field. It is, of course, not feasible here to attempt a summary of each of the informative articles. The book itself testifies to the serious attention which scholars have devoted to the subject in the decade of the sixties, and it is a precursor of a host of studies which will reach the public in the seventies. Neubeck states his own conclusion simply: "It is now clear that marriage can work out successfully for both of the spouses even when it is not an all-inclusive relationship, when either in reality or in fantasy there are other persons who share one's life" (pp. 23–24).

" " " " "

It is noteworthy in the foregoing brief survey that there is a movement from the love elite to extramarital relations among various classes of people. Any person who is aware of contemporary culture cannot miss the increasing attention given to the subject in newspaper feature articles, popular magazines, the movies, television, professional journals, the theater, novels, music lyrics, programs at professional conferences, and unpublished graduate theses. We know of at least twenty researchers producing books and articles on the subject, and undoubtedly others are adding to the rapidly growing literature (see suggested reading for chapter five). We agree with the conviction of Rustum and Della Roy previously quoted: "We foresee an inevitable and rapid increase in such co-marital relationships." And though we also agree with them wholeheartedly that it is "the Church's urgent business to provide guidelines for the most creative conduct within [co-marital relationships]," we would go further and say it is the time for all men and women who value the enrichment of multirelational intimacy, regardless of their marital status, to act and speak out with integrity and without shame.

It is, unfortunately, not the case that women and men groping for new marital lifestyles can, will, or feel free to act or speak according to the values they seek to realize in their lives. It is one thing to cite studies of the subject; another to confront the reality where each person lives, moves, and has his/her being. Explorations in unconventional patterns of sexual intimacy can cause intense personal uncertainty, anguish, or risk.

A man in his late twenties looks resolutely at the small group of couples around him and quietly shatters the security of conversational generalizations by saying, "Well, I personally think it's a good way to live because I would feel less than a free man if my marriage meant I couldn't have other close friends of the opposite sex." The reactions of the group are varied, but the risk-taking of this man who has a professional practice in a conservative Bible Belt community is impressive. His wife emphasizes his testimony with a reassuring smile and by placing her hand in his. Others then begin to share their own previously unexpressed feelings, doubts, and needs, and the seminar turns into a moving experience for the group.

During an adult discussion session in a midwest household, a woman in her early forties, a professor married to a lawyer, suddenly vents her anger and frustration: "Dammit, why do John and I have to feel like freaks just because we'd like to be close with other people?" The response that countless other couples in all parts of the country are also searching for warm extramarital relationships, is not reassuring to her.

A counseling client in Massachusetts, a librarian in her late thirties, clarifies her situation with a sense of accomplishment by saying, "I didn't plan on having an open-ended marriage. It simply began to develop that way when I discovered that my husband loves other women besides me; that he's not monogamous in a traditional way. This realization freed me from the obscenity of possessiveness. Some of my extramarital relationships have been fruitful to me and I'm less naïvely open with others, but no less free. I do wonder about the future—there's a measure of risk and uncertainty in the way we've now chosen, but I'm learning not to be afraid to be a person, a woman with worthwhile contributions to make to human society. As a matter of fact, there is a continual excitement about our marital relationship and mutual growing—anything else would be emotional death for us."

One of the reasons why relational innovators experience so much agony, shame, and confusion is that, in our society, the traditional model of monogamous marriage is assumed to be self-validating. It is even sanctified in the wedding ceremony by the promise to forsake all others and keep one's self for the spouse only. Yet, if anything is more obvious about the present plight of the family, it is that something is radically wrong with our expectations about, preparations for, and behavior within marriage. We refer not only to the high number of divorces, separations, and desertions, but to the emotional torture, the violence toward spouse and children, the unhappiness and quiet desperation which characterize so many marriages. If this marital carnage were simply a result of individual character weakness and moral degeneracy then religious revivals would perhaps provide the solution. It is, however, the very model of marriage itself which needs emergency treatment and rehabilitation through change of function. Even including the values of parenthood, marriage cannot provide us with, nor does it exhaust, the meaning of our lives. It is a stereotyped form of living which is overrated. Certainly, we are not advocating an end to marriage or the family, nor are we claiming that marriage is not without great worth. On the contrary, healthy marriage is a source of immense joy and fulfillment when it provides a context for human growth, strength, and freedom; when it sustains separateness as well as mutuality; uniqueness and privacy as well as community and sharing. Marriage is a difficult accomplishment, and it is not for everyone; at least it ought not to be routinely expected that everyone should commit himself to it by age twenty-five—or even thirty. Marriage requires more than romantic love and good sex, as delightful and important as they are. It requires self-actualizing persons who have direction or purpose in life, who can function creatively under the tension between commitment and freedom.

Marriage between two with the intention of lifetime commitment will continue to be the predominant model of marital union in our culture for generations. It merits our care and rebuilding not only because it exists, but because there are enduring values to a one-to-one primary relationship which cannot easily be supplanted. One such value is continuity in relational experience. Even as we learn to love because we are loved, to trust because we are trusted, we continue to actualize our being in relation to a responding other whose responses we understand and respect. There is much painful learning in the give and take of mutual growth, and the constancy of this relationship is crucial to our evaluation of who and what we are. There is, too, the sheer exuberance in being appreciated for who we are: with pimples as well as attractiveness; with hangups as well as uninhibited passion; with weakness as well as virtues; with failures as well as achievements. There is an incomparably satisfying happiness in knowing and being known; in loving and being loved; in giving help and receiving help; in sharing a myriad of emotions. When we consider the possible benefits and enrichments of one-to-one commitment, it should not be surprising that male or female homosexual lovers not subject to conventional pressures to marry, should also desire to unite their lives through public testimony, religious ceremony, and legal matrimony.

Traditional monogamy, however, no longer provides for mutual self-realization. We consider traditional monogamy, with its rigid requirement for exclusive devotion and affection, even though hallowed by the theological concept of fidelity, to be a culturally approved mass neurosis. It should be clearly understood that we do not deny anyone the freedom to enter conventional marriage—an absolute covenant between two persons of the opposite sex. Each person has the freedom to make decisions for life affirmation according to his/her deepest convictions and highest priorities, and sometimes what may outwardly appear to be merely a conventional form of marriage may be for the two people involved the epitome of love, joy, and hope. It is possible for a man and a woman to be content and happy only with each other and family members. Indeed, we support all the efforts of various human relations disciplines to strengthen and make more rewarding conventional monogamy. What we do emphatically reject, however, is our society's sanction of this marital model as normative and supreme. We believe all civic and constitutional rights should be extended to personal lifestyles. We prefer a model of monogamy which celebrates co-marital intimacy and does not equate fidelity with sexual exclusiveness. For too long, traditional moralists have been passively allowed to pre-empt other conscientious lifestyles by propagating the unproven assumptions that we cannot love more than one person (of the opposite sex) concurrently; that co-marital or extramarital sex always destroys marriage; that "good" marriages are totally self-contained and self-restrictive and sufficient; that only emotionally unstable people seek and need intimate relationships outside the husband-wife bond. We repudiate these assumptions and consider them half-truths at best. When these assumptions are dogmatically upheld by society as eternal truths we consider the phenomenon to be a cultural neurosis in the sense that the issue is predetermined, all nonconformists are castigated, and there is no openness to new experience in new contexts.

The semantics of conformity are intimidating. Relational innovators are constantly accosted with negative terms such as promiscuity, adultery, and infidelity. Even the books previously cited use these terms in a haphazard and confusing manner. The word "promiscuous," for example, refers to people who lack standards of selection, who are indiscriminate in sexual relations. It should be obvious that it's possible for a person to be sexually intimate with any number of persons chosen according to conscientious standards. The word is commonly used, however, as a judgment against anyone who has more than one socially approved sexual relationship, and especially in a double-standard way against women. This shows a mistaken emphasis on the quantity rather than the quality of interpersonal relationships. It also insists that people cannot have casual sexual experiences. Not all intimate relationships must have the same intensity. Millions of men and women are able to make rapid appraisals of others with whom they can exchange warmth without subsequent emotional strings attached.

Even the term "extramarital" is misleading in the context

of open-ended marriage. For it is precisely *within* marriage rather than outside it that open-ended marriage incorporates the freedom for two spouses to enjoy multilateral sexual and friendship relations. "Extramarital" is an all-encompassing term referring to all forms of relationship, usually sexual, with partners other than the spouse. "Co-marital" is a more appropriate term for open-ended marriages because it at least carries the connotations of togetherness and co-operation within the structure of the marriage. Persons participating in an open-ended marriage covenant not only with each other, but with the Family of Man. In a profound sense all children are their children, and all adults are their loved ones. Within such marriages the possibility of adultery is totally absent because exclusion, possessiveness, and jealousy have no place in the relationship. "Adultery" is a theological judgment which can apply only to the restrictive type of covenant. When one partner breaks the vow of "to thee only do I promise to keep myself," a relationship of trust is broken and he or she is unfaithful. But it's also possible to create a model of marriage—a covenant—monogamous in the sense that it's based upon an intended lifetime commitment between two, but which nevertheless is open-ended because it does not exclude the freedom to have any number of intimate relationships with others. The phrase "adultery with consent" is occasionally used by scholars simply because we do not yet have the language to reflect new relational models. But "adultery with consent" is a contradiction in terms. The only way adultery can be committed is to betray a covenant of mutual trust based on sexual exclusiveness. A good example of this understandable semantic confusion is contained in this statement by Dr. Eugene Scheimann of Chicago:

" " " " "

I have seen adultery with consent add a rich, new dimension to the lives of couples who believe that sex with more than one person is enjoyable. As the years go by, these couples long to feel again the touch of a new body and the spark of a new personality, yet they nevertheless have a commitment to their marriage partner that makes them want to be totally honest with each other. In any event, this new emphasis on honesty and sex sharing can be seen as a part of the cultural revolution our society is now undergoing.[11]

// // // // //

What Dr. Scheimann sees with his clients is not a new kind of adultery, but a movement beyond adultery, and the words of Rustum and Della Roy are wise counsel: "It is important to avoid words such as *adultery.*"

"Infidelity" is, unfortunately, commonly used as a synonym for "adultery." The open-ended marriage which respects the integrity of the other and which values sexual liberty transcends adultery but takes infidelity seriously because the criteria of unfaithfulness are more important than sexual behavior. Unfaithfulness in creative marriage—or, for that matter, in any friendship relationship—has to do with constriction of love; with false security; with lack of respect for the equality of the other's personhood; with suffocating possessiveness which is life-denying. There are so many ways to be unfaithful to one another in a nonsexual sense. Unfaithfulness in human relationships effectively means the denial of a relationship; it is a lack of trust and honesty; it is based on fear of the other and an uncertainty about self; it has a thousand faces. It is not that people must be perfect in their relationships—all of us fail each other at times. But those who can only understand conventional morality fail to recognize and acknowledge the values of those who take infidelity in human relationships seriously while at the same time refusing to constrict themselves to exclusive intimacy.

It is ironic and hypocritical—perhaps even unconstitutional—for courts to grant divorce on the grounds of adultery while refusing to accept and honor the testimony of couples who wish divorce on the grounds of mutual incompatibility, or unhappiness, or on irreconcilable infidelity in the broader, nonsexual sense. Why should the state recognize only one kind of religious marriage covenant (sexual exclusiveness) and not grant divorce status to others, married under different covenants, who find they cannot live together according to their hopes and intentions? This is a possible violation of the principle of separation of church and state, and divorce law reformers should challenge the state's right to make such arbitrary moral judgments. Curiously, even Hollywood continues to be conservative in this respect. In defense of a controversial film, the president of the Motion Picture Association of America declared with self-evident justification: "Everyone in the film who takes part in adultery comes to a horrible end. It was a beautiful picture."[12]

The open-ended marriage is certainly monogamous—a primary one-to-one relationship based on mutual commitment and intended to last for a lifetime. In this sense, it is quite conventional. It is not, however, based on a covenant exclusive of other intimate and sensual friendships. It even may or may not involve formal marriage. But unlike others who see the marriage ceremony as only a convenience of the state for the protection of children's rights and for the registration of familial and property claims, we see values in an open proclamation of mutual commitment through some public act or religious ceremony. Such an event is a wonderful opportunity to share private meanings with cherished friends, to celebrate the creation of love, and to rejoice openly in the promise of a new life venture.

We are not unaware of, or insensitive to, the tremendous risks and hard challenges to human growth which are necessarily involved in an open-ended marriage. It's essential to realize that an unknown but significant number of men and women are ready and eager to face these risks and challenges because they are aware that a more joyful and loving marital lifestyle is possible and attainable. It's time for family life educators and counselors to take the goal of marriage with sexual liberty seriously and empathically, for what we wish to eradicate in relationships has value for all marriage. We want to eradicate the resentment born of the double standard and maintained by male supremacists; the hostility and jealousy tearing men and women apart emotionally if not physically; the possessiveness stifling human growth; the deceit of adultery which makes hypocrisy an art, cheapens integrity, and makes honesty with children impossible.

What a new model of open-ended marriage seeks to promote is risk-taking in trust; the warmth of loving without anxiety; the extension of affection; the excitement and pleasure of knowing sensuously a variety of other persons; the enrichment which personalities can contribute to each other; the joy of being fully alive in every encounter.

# CHAPTER TWO / THE DOUBLE STANDARD
## AND PEOPLE'S LIBERATION

O O O O O O O O O O O O O O O O O O O O O O O O O O
O O O O O O O O O O O O O O O O O O O O O O O O O O
O O O O O O O O O O O O O O O O O O O O O O O O O O
O O O O O O O O O O O O O O O O O O O O O O O O O O
O O O O O O O O O O O O O O O O O O O O O O O O O O
O O O O O O O O O O O O O O O O O O O O O O O O O O
O O O O O O O O O O O O O O O O O O O O O O O O O O
O O O O O O O O O O O O O O O O O O O O O O O O O O
O O O O O O O O O O O O O O O O O O O O O O O O O O

The term "double standard" is commonly applied to a specific area of the human condition: namely, the sexual; and even more specifically, to premarital sexual behavior and standards. Sociological analysis keeps the public preoccupied with the number of people, or the percentage of a prescribed population, which may be engaged in a given category (behavior, opinion, change, or relationship). The focus on quantitative factors is central to the lively (and sometimes ridiculous) controversy among the professionals as to whether the contemporary sexual scene should be classified as revolutionary, evolutionary, or status quo–maintaining. Our obsession with charting incidences of sexual behavior and counting orgasms is a kind of cultural voyeurism. Since we are not about to expose ourselves in honest behavior we would rather peek into other people's lives and live vicariously. We can also have fun by condemning or shaming others who challenge our particular version of decency. And finally, after we count enough heads and watch cautiously until the creative becomes commonplace, we can then safely leap into our cipher in the mass and enjoy a new experience. In the expression of our sexual desires, hopes, and needs, most of us are moral cowards.

The double standard as such is not necessarily cowardly. On the contrary, it is a *standard* which many men and women willingly accept if not choose. But what we fail to realize is that there is in fact a multiplicity of sexual standards operative in America. The major issue is not the quantitative weight of any one standard over another, but the quality of interpersonal relationships to be realized within any one of the standards. In our society, which is struggling to provide greater freedom for a broad variety of sexual standards and lifestyles (sexual pluralism), it is any person's privilege and right to live by the double standard. What must be rejected, however, is the tyranny of the standard when it is imposed upon those who repudiate it for their own lives and who see its destructiveness on those young men and women who are kept ignorant of other options for contemporary man-woman relationships.

Although there are indications that the double standard is on the decline, it is by no means dead and it continues to provide, for better or for worse, countless young people with both the ground rules for sexual behavior and the framework for masculine and feminine roles. Speaking of present-day premarital sexual standards, sociologist Ira Reiss[1] believes that there are four major types: Abstinence for both sexes; the Double Standard defined as "the Western world's oldest standard, which allows males to have greater access to coitus than females"; Permissiveness with Affection, an increasingly popular acceptance of intercourse for both sexes when a warm and stable relationship prevails; and Permissiveness without Affection which allows both sexes equal sexual experience even in relationships which require only mutual consent without emotional strings attached. Regardless of how influential other standards may become, and no matter how many creative variations may be developed, it is likely that the double standard will continue to shape relationships for a large number of people into the foreseeable future. For in addition to providing sex-role models and defining the privileges and penalties for the behavior of both sexes, the double standard is tacitly condoned by both Judaism and Christianity; social institutions provide for its perpetuation; the education establishment promotes it; and a host of myths reinforce it. The double standard rests on the assumption that sex pleasure is not for everyone and that men need it more and know best how to enjoy it while protecting their women from its hazards. Such protection is, of course, "necessary" to uphold the moral order, to make women happy, and to preserve the family. These are the deeply held convictions of many men and women who see the double standard as a small price to pay for the sake of such worthy goals.

Again, the problem essentially is not that there are people who hold to the double standard; it is that our society incorporates and sanctions it and persecutes in various ways those who conscientiously hold other standards and seek to live alternative or nonconventional lifestyles. It is also important to recognize that the double standard of sexual morality permeates vital areas of intimate relationships other than just the premarital. Consequently, the person who repudiates double standardism finds that a social web of conformity creates sticky problems in several areas of interpersonal encounter.

*Single Men Versus Single Women.* As has been noted, premarital sexual behavior draws a great deal of attention and concern in our society. It is almost as if men and women are embarrassed to seem interested in sexual pleasure once they are married. Much safer is it to use the children as the focal point for adult interest in sex. True, there are obvious legitimate concerns such as pregnancy, venereal disease, and social ostracism. We also make a tremendous emotional and financial investment in our children and dread the "ruination" of their lives through sexual folly. But the hazards of premarital sex go beyond these fears and even beyond the traditional risks of the double standard penalties. The ground rules of the double standard are shifting in a gradual but devastating way with the female being trapped in a double bind: if she is sexually inexperienced she is "out of it"; if she takes her sexual freedom seriously, she is "trash," or, at best, not "the kind of a woman that I'd want to be the mother of my children." The usual penalties imposed upon the female under the double standard result in higher incidences of guilt on the occasion of the first intimacy; lower incidences of masturbation; and the indictment of "promiscuous" applied almost exclusively to them while corresponding male behavior is considered "adventure," "experience," "conquest," and "virile." Where this type of double standard now really begins to destroy male-female communication and compatible mutual game playing is *after* the period of engagement. Whereas previously the relationship of engagement signalized permission for sexual exploration and experimentation, it is now becoming a deed which the male uses to claim exclusive rights to the female who, in turn, is required to end her intimate relationships with all other male friends and lovers in order to devote herself solely to the "winner" of her body. It is becoming more common for young men not to be at all bothered by or about the premarital sexual experience of their girlfriends, but they are still playing a game of conquest and possession. With great cool, gentleness, and *joie de vivre*, the pseudo-liberated single male relates sympathetically to the single female who is struggling for autonomous identity and sexual freedom. This promising communion between the sexes is, however, short-lived, for as soon as that emancipated young woman consents to a primary one-to-one commitment, the double standard heart of the male beats mightily and he suffocates the flame of love with possessiveness and jealousy. This is not to say that only males are possessive and jealous, but in the premarital stage they are becoming more devious about it, victims of their own con game. With justifiable bitterness, Shulamith Firestone, in *Dialectic of Sex*, excoriates the deceptions of male-designed sexual freedom which does nothing more than provide the men with a greater supply of free lays: "The rhetoric of the sexual revolution, if it brought no improvement for women, proved to have great value for men. By convincing women that the usual female games and demands were despicable, unfair, prudish, old-fashioned, puritanical, and self-destructive, a new reservoir of available females was created to expand the tight supply of goods available for traditional sexual exploitation, disarming women of even the little protection they had so painfully acquired . . . (but) even the hippest want an 'old lady' who is relatively unused."[2]

The above kind of delayed double standard double cross is not yet common in our culture and is more likely to occur in urban colleges than among other young adult populations in this country. Indeed, young adults in certain geographical regions and social classes would still consider the old-fashioned prerogative of sex-with-engagement (Permissiveness with Affection) as being daring and radical. There is also another population of young men and women, small but growing in number, who are sexually liberated and doing a new thing together as they develop an equalitarian standard of sexual morality. But it is disheartening to see how adaptable the destructive aspects of the premarital double standard can be: the value of virginity is being rejected, only to be replaced by the delayed arbitrary judgment and possessiveness of the male, and young adults of both sexes still face the bleak prospect of continued mutual manipulation.

*Parents Versus Children.* Another form of the sexual double standard which can be destructive is embodied in the myth which declares that sex is only for adults. There is assumed to be a magical moment of maturity beyond which sex is mentionable and before which it is simply not acknowledged as an essential human experience. Though parents by and large favor some form of sex education in public and religious schools, their naïveté is nevertheless incredible. Too little is offered much too late: it is as if parents refuse to recognize their children as sexual and sensual beings. Children, of course, tend to reciprocate the insult and find it hard to believe that their parents, and adults in general, can participate in and enjoy sexual intimacy. It is sad when children lack adult models who express emotional warmth and playful physical closeness, who admit to a lively interest in sex. Too many parents not only conceal their earthiness, but even worry about their children or make them feel ashamed when they exhibit or acknowledge an interest in sex. Parents tend to feel uncomfortable talking to their children about sex unless they can tell jokes on the one hand, or, on the other, speak in ethereal, poetic, or religious terms.

Fortunately, some progress has been made in sex education in the last generation or two. It is now undoubtedly rare for parents to conduct a bedcheck to make sure the child is sleeping on his back with arms outside the blankets lest the unspeakable vice be committed in the unguarded moments of sleep. Masturbation is generally understood and accepted as a natural process of self-discovery and self-enjoyment, and children today are spared the shame ard hangups which not too long ago were the horrendous heritage of most men and women. Curiously, however, parents and educators consider the lack of condemnation of masturbation sufficient to the educational needs of young people. This is still a negative approach to the subject, for a more honest and helpful service to children would be to make sure that all girls and boys, by the end of the seventh grade at least, were made aware of the positive and beneficial aspects of masturbation: benefits such as relaxation of physical and psychic tension, comfortableness with sensuality, self-knowledge and self-acceptance, and empathy with the sexual need of the other sex.[3] Even at the present time, this is still too much to ask of most parents because it is so difficult for adults to accept and feel comfortable with the sexual needs and development of children. It is amazing how much can be blocked out of adult memories! If parents themselves did not initiate a double standard which creates a make-believe world of nonsexual children, they would experience less anxiety about their children's behavior and would be privileged with greater sharing from young people who, regardless of new attitudes toward sex, are still searching for honest and creative relationships. To be sure, the problems of sex education and permissible sexual behavior for young people are complex and involve more than the parental double standard. But a start must be made somewhere with realistic and forthright education for human sexuality—education which adults need as much as children. How this will be accomplished on a wide social scale is yet unclear and even a controversial issue. One interesting proposal, by Harriet F. Pilpel, general counsel for Planned Parenthood–World Population, is that the sex education needs and civil rights of children should be protected by law and be taken as seriously as the rights of parents and society. She suggests that ombudsmen be appointed to speak for children and is convinced that "adequately serving children's needs also serves the best interests of their parents and community" (SIECUS Newsletter, October 1970). Perhaps we wouldn't need some official to speak on behalf of children if parents and educators had the courage and sensitivity to help them appreciate without fear their own being—genitals included.

*Husbands Versus Wives.* In light of the fact that the overwhelming majority of men and women marry, it may seem preposterous for serious scholars of family life to wonder if marriage has a future. Yet, a long-time observer of man-woman relationships, sociologist Jessie Bernard, states frankly that marriage is a poor status for women and she offers the startling proposal that celibacy be considered as an honorable alternate status for women.[4] And in almost every major popular family magazine today, there are articles detailing the troubled condition of the institution of marriage. One of the major forces relentlessly demanding a re-evaluation and reformulation of the marital relationship is the Women's Liberation Movement—a resurgence of the feminist movement which won the voting franchise and then seemingly dissipated by 1930. The new Movement, though diffuse and eclectic, has a cohesive and radical cutting edge which will not be blunted in its effectiveness until human relationships and society are reshaped to allow all women full self-realization as persons.

Because of the work of the Women's Liberation Movement, the double standardism of male chauvinists and their co-opted female victims has been mercilessly exposed. The scholars and leaders of the Movement have amassed a devastating indictment of the male's total cultural and personal ego trip—a trip made on the free-to-all-men ticket of the double standard. It is interesting to note that discussion of the double standard by psychologists, sociologists, and other professionals has mostly been confined to premarital behavior and rarely analyzed in any depth. The Encyclopedia of Sexual Behavior, for example, includes no article on the subject and cites only three minor references to the double standard in the index.[5] It is remarkable how sensitive most aware adults are to the issues of the double standard considering the fact that it is only within the last several years that women in any significant number began again a revolt against their inane condition. As recently as 1964, in her comprehensive analysis of the status of women, Alice S. Rossi could say, regrettably, "There is no overt antifeminism in our society in 1964, not because sex equality has been achieved, but because there is practically no feminist spark left among American women."[6] Betty Friedan's *The Feminine Mystique* (1963) had not yet made its impact, but it didn't take long for the awakening of the American woman. It is disturbing that six turbulent years after sociologist Rossi's understated challenge, two male sociologists would claim that "the role of women has changed very little, and today they are even more committed to the home and children than they were in the 1930's during the last gasp of feminism."[7] Feminism did not, however, die in the 1930s. It merely smoldered until the secret spark was bellowed into a roaring and hot movement by Friedan and her colleagues. After handling hot steel during the war years of the 1940s, women again were faced with a bitter reality. Men determine the purposes and structure of social institutions, define sex roles, judge sexual behavior, set the conditions for economic independence, commit all physical and human resources to national priorities which they determine, and on top of it all evaluate the sanity of women. It is no wonder that almost all men know in their hearts at least one prayer: "I thank thee, Lord (ol' Buddy), that I was not born a woman!"

One of the critical questions the Movement poses relates to the impact it will have upon husband-wife relationships. No definitive answer is yet possible, but a reasonable guess is that the Movement will cause more trouble than peace, at least for a transitional period. The number of divorces and unhappy marriages is evidence that husband-wife warfare is rampant, and consciousness-raising sessions aren't going to make women any happier with their predicaments. Ultimately, the Movement will contribute to the humanization of both sexes, but for the time being it must risk the opening of festering hates and resentments in marital relations. Men have been the exclusive objects of devotion by mothers who knew no better, and adult males unconsciously expect to occupy the place of the deity in the lives of their wives. There are even a sufficient number of wives who exalt this juvenile expectation to the status of "true love." Men and women who accept the double-standard marriage can share a common value framework and make each other content within that context. But even this is becoming more difficult to accomplish, for the traditional uneasy truce which suffers adulterous cheating on the part of the husband is about to break down because women are weary of the hypocrisy and are more willing to face the consequences of painful marital confrontation. Husbands do continue to have the upper hand, for all the world loves a lover (male), and the wife who is so crass as to object is a "bitch," while the wife who is independent enough to have her own male friends and night out is a "whore." Women who are relatively happy with the way things are will bitterly resent the Movement for raising issues they would rather not confront. Not all women seek the same kind of liberation, and it will be important for the Movement not to alienate needlessly those women who choose to maintain the status quo for their lives and their marriages.

The leaders of Women's Liberation are prepared for a male countermovement and are consolidating for survival. Their expectations of male reprisals may not be unfounded, and if their analysis of the extent of female subjugation is correct, it can be anticipated that the radical aspects of the Movement will be totally ignored if not suppressed. There is, however, another small but determined movement in our society which repudiates the double standard of sexual morality and is a strong supporter of the liberation of women in all areas of society; this is the Movement for Alternative Lifestyles.

The Movement for Alternative Lifestyles is more amorphous and eclectic than the Women's Liberation Movement and it doesn't even merit capital letters and a grand name. But it's for real and it's changing the lives of people and will eventually make permanent changes in American social institutions. This movement, discussed in greater detail in chapter five, includes such experiments in sexual freedom and interpersonal relations as: *noncontractual cohabitation*, so-called trial marriages, a version of which is finding an accepted place in co-ed dormitories on various campuses; *group marriage*, in which three or more persons create a marital covenant with every other member of the group; *communes*, in which married couples and/or single persons share living resources and also accept mutual responsibilities for community but without necessarily permitting group sex or partner sharing; and *swinging*, so-called spouse swapping, which promotes the kind of group sex which couples participate in together but with a minimum of emotional commitment to the other couples. Styles can, of course, be combined into several variations. Another less well known option or alternative in marital patterns is the *open-ended marriage,* with which this book is concerned.

Fundamental to all of the new options, however, is the conviction that women have an equal right to sexual experimentation, satisfaction, and freedom. And where single-standard restrictions are valued, voluntarily accepted, and self-disciplined, the male also has an equal responsibility to maintain the same values and behavior as his partner. Ultimately, it is a profound yet joyful quality of sexual intimacy and interpersonal sharing which husbands and wives are seeking for themselves, each other, and for their friends through new lifestyles.

*Heterosexuals Versus Homosexuals.* In no other aspect of sexual behavior is the double standard more vicious than in the conflict between heterosexuals and homosexuals. This conflict is commonly presented in terms of normalcy versus deviancy, but this framework itself is a propaganda success of heterosexuals. What is universal or normal in human sexual behavior is for two persons to need each other for mutual sensual enjoyment. Nothing in human nature requires that two persons engaged in such pleasure be of different sexes. Human beings are human beings, and however they may please, comfort, support, inspire, or love each other is of human value. Though it is unusual in our culture for persons to direct sexual passion, with or without love, to members of the same sex, such behavior and relationships can contribute to the mental and physical well-being of both persons involved. Wherever and however two people touch across their loneliness to satisfy their needs, a human event takes place. Heterosexuals set for themselves exceedingly high expectations and standards of sexual fulfillment, but they deny homosexuals the same rights and opportunities. Because of customary religious condemnation, cultural conditioning, the threat of the unusual, and personal hangups, we prefer to assign homosexuality to the

realm of the perverse and the pathological. It is ironic that
the prejudice against homosexuals should provide common
ground for some clergymen and psychiatrists who otherwise
would have little to say to each other. The Victorian moral-
izing of a few psychiatrists makes them sound like preachers
and anti-homosexuality crusaders. Even the modern "apostle
of sane sex," Dr. David Reuben, writes on the subject of
homosexuality with a pseudo-scientific moralism, thereby
justifying those who were afraid to ask in the first place.[8]
Though his opinions are expressed with sarcastic humor rather
than melodramatic Victorian self-righteousness, Dr. Reuben
presents a grossly distorted view of same sex behavior. His
outrageous generalizations about the character and motivation
of homosexuals are based on his selection of case studies,
second-hand reports, and medical gossip, all of which involve
bizarre behavior or psychopathology to begin with, and he
completely omits any discussion of homosexuals who are
emotionally healthy and creative. The entire presentation is
without compassion or empathy, shallow in understanding,
and a cruel caricature of homosexuals. It is to be hoped that
this Krafft-Ebing type of catalogue of sexual horrors will no
longer frighten or shame people into conformist behavior.

One of the experiments in sexual freedom which will
eventually bridge the tensions and distinctions between homosexuals and heterosexuals is the phenomenon of group sex as
a form of play. The John Birch Society and the Christian
Crusade evangelicals were perceptive when they shifted their
coordinated and massive attack against sex education in the
schools to a campaign against sensitivity training in the
schools. When significant numbers of people become involved
with the widespread encounter/sensitivity training movement,
unpredictable changes are bound to occur in people and society. If men and women shed inhibitions, risk openness and
intimacy through touching, and discover the pleasures of
shameless sensuality, then all of the familiar protocols of sexual behavior soon become questioned and challenged. In effect,

people become less afraid to exhibit and receive physical affection. That such a cultural development can be considered dangerous to established morality and American civilization is a commentary on the impoverishment and fragility of our venerable values—or at least on the way in which those values are being interpreted. The ultraconservatives are at least more prophetic in their alarm than are the liberals who, in their analytical supercool, quibble about the precise degree of social change. The encounter/sensitivity movement, in spite of its potential dangers to any unwary individual who cannot cope with its personalized impact, is creating a new class of sensually adventurous persons; men and women who rejoice in their flesh-and-bloodness; who delight in mutual exchanges of being-with-you-in-the-flesh pleasure; who affirm their sensual condition without shame. Sexual playfulness for such persons is a more creative and zestful way of living than the self-stultification which so many people face as their fate. Instead of the overbearing ogling of males or the come-on twittering of frustrated females, a more honest delight in mutual sensual exploration is possible. The essence of the sexual revolution is not revealed in the statistics of who-does-what-to-whom-how-many-times; it is in the new attitude of sex as play and the willingness of people to act accordingly. It is probable that only a very small percent of those who have had "growth group" experience will experiment with group sex. Of that number there will be those who decide that this type of activity is not their thing. Others, however, will discover that they have a capacity for sensual enjoyment with members of the same sex as well as with those of the different sex. It can be a discovery which is mind expanding and spirit freeing—a dazzling escape from emotional captivity which leads to sweet freedom in a new world. Suddenly, the sexual population is no longer divided into only two types, heterosexuals and homosexuals, with their respective stereotyped roles. To become a *bisexual* is to discover the joy of relating with sensual affection to those of one's own sex, and astonishingly, those people who were once impersonal competitors are now potentially personal friends; it is to discover the other half of humanity of which the self is part. And by experiencing one's own homosexual potential, homosexuals no longer seem queer, for now we can empathize with their feelings without threat to our own masculinity or femininity. The variety of sexual patterns increases and enriches all. Instead of only two styles in opposition to each other, we have a range of behaviors:

exclusive heterosexuality
bisexuality with dominant heterosexuality
bisexuality with dominant homosexuality
exclusive homosexuality

These categories could undoubtedly be refined (see chapter five). Are there, for example, people who are bisexual with equal preferences? Is it possible for a given individual to move through two or all of these categories at different phases of her/his life? As usual, the language of sex becomes a problem, and descriptive phrases can sound awkward. Even definitions are not uniform. The term "bisexual," for instance, can refer to a hermaphrodite, a person born with both male and female organs. Its use here, of course, refers to a person who experiences sexual intimacy with others of each sex.

*Beyond the Double Standard.* The double standard of morality has lost its pre-eminent status in contemporary human relationships, but it will long exist to some degree in some form or other. Perhaps no other standard will take its place, for the present challenge is not so much to replace it with one ideal substitute, but to create a social climate which fosters pluralism in sex standards and allows for experimentation in lifestyle. The varieties of sexual expression and the meanings each individual attaches to his/her experience are incalculable. Tension between standards will not be eradicated and people will continue to feel conflict with each other, but the tension can be creative and the conflicts can be growth opportunities if we could learn to value differences and to appreciate each other's humanity. Even sexual freedom can rigidify and become oppressive if the people who consider themselves liberated become pridefully intolerant of the values, preferences, and conditions of others. The British psychologist Derek Wright raised a valid issue in a *Life* magazine editorial (November 6, 1970) when he wrote on "the new tyranny of sexual liberation." In that provocative article he warns: "We begin to grade our sexual partners, as they us, though we do not talk about it. And standards are rising. Too often for the sex experts, the merely possible is instantly the optimal, and tomorrow, for the rest of us, the normal. How we pity or scorn the impotent and the frigid! While, absurdly, some people use sex to exorcise their insecurities, others who find it difficult, distasteful or merely dull conclude that they are odd, outcast and, most desolating of all, inadequate. It is so easy to build a prison around a man by convincing him he is a prisoner." Even among the supposedly sexually enlightened the grading often takes place. It is dismaying how persons who are sensitive, informed, and experienced will nevertheless have stereotyped expectations of the sexual responses of a partner. If technical performance (for example, strength of erection of clitoris, nipples, or penis; timing and intensity of orgasm or ejaculation; level of excitement and response to certain stimuli; endurance in certain positions, etc.) does not conform to textbook standards or does not measure up to prior encounters of memorable climax, then disappointment, doubt, or analytical probing ruin the pleasure of the experience. The sheer delight in being naked together and appreciating the specialness of the moment, the joy of intimacy, the sharing of sensuality can be entirely missed by those who are preoccupied with the end result of the Big O. Yes, there is tremendous value in being knowledgeable about the usual sexual responses of men and women; it is important to anticipate the needs and desires of your partner and to bring him/her to complete satisfaction when possible and desired.

But this type of expertise need not be the focus of the experience—it can be the background which enriches the pleasure and value of two (or more) persons creating a beautiful time of affirmation and affection. The combinations and varieties of level of lust, genital intensity, orgasmic patterns, physiological endowments, mood on the occasion, etc., are endless, and every act of intimacy is unique, never to be precisely duplicated. Enjoyable sex requires relaxed humor and the ability to appreciate the wonder of the moment on whatever level it can honestly be felt.

To go beyond the double standard, then, it is required of us that we be autonomous, to stand on our own values, to resist enslavement by any sex ideology, and to focus on whole persons as well as on genitals. Of society, it is required that the conditions for, and rights of, sexual freedom be established and upheld in order that all standards and lifestyles may be practiced as long as they do no violence to individuals or interfere with the civil rights of others. This task is overwhelming but possible of accomplishment if enough people will work to shape a social order which holds human well-being and community as high national priorities. The quality of personal lives cannot be enriched within a dehumanizing social environment; society cannot be radically reformed without men and women who are willing to act with courage. Professor Arnold Birenbaum of Wheaton College (Mass.) captures the interdependence of self and society in relation to sexuality with the observation that "The failure to achieve an independent sexual life, as part of an independent personality, is the result of the absence of any society-wide effort to bring about the removal of the fragmenting character of modern society. To create the autonomous personality, we must put an end to conditions which produce self-estrangement. The effort itself must involve the self in all its complexity, otherwise the sexual revolution only serves to continue the sense of helplessness, bewilderment, loneliness, and self-estrangement. It cannot be done for us but only by us."⁹

In other words, the issues of sexual values, relationships, and behavior cannot be isolated from the political, economic, racial, and other critical issues of our time. The search for happy sex is ultimately self-destructive if it is not related to the context of total human sexuality and the search for the meaning of life. The social action of homosexuals and lesbians, for example, is redeeming for them as human beings and redeeming for society, which is humanized in the process of response and change. Their sexuality is affirmed ("I am a whole male/female person!") and the restoration of dignity gives them greater meaning in life ("I will not hide in shame, I can contribute to society!"). The humane and reconciling approach and the constructive recommendations of the final report on homosexuality of the National Institute of Mental Health (October 1969) is a hopeful example of the fact that sexual prejudice and myths can be overcome and social policy transformed, once enlightened women and men apply themselves to the task. Of course, the implementation of that report remains to be accomplished.

In any case, before we can achieve a national condition of liberated people—men, women, and children—the hard issues raised by the Women's Liberation Movement will have to be faced and resolved honestly and directly. There is no getting around it. The Movement is serious and will not fade away, and all people will benefit from its reformation of human communion and community.

# CHAPTER THREE / NEEDED: NEW ATTITUDES TOWARD INTIMACY

O O O O O O O O O O O O O O O O O O O O O O O O
O O O O O O O O O O O O O O O O O O O O O O O O
O O O O O O O O O O O O O O O O O O O O O O O O
O O O O O O O O O O O O O O O O O O O O O O O O
O O O O O O O O O O O O O O O O O O O O O O O O
O O O O O O O O O O O O O O O O O O O O O O O O
O O O O O O O O O O O O O O O O O O O O O O O O
O O O O O O O O O O O O O O O O O O O O O O O O
O O O O O O O O O O O O O O O O O O O O O O O O

## UNDERSTANDING THE NEED FOR SEX EDUCATION OF YOUTH

The intense sex education controversy of the 1960s—so clearly sketched in the book *Oh, Sex Education*, by Mary Breasted,[1] is a controversy which is by no means over. It may be less hysterical and vicious, but complicated—and perhaps unresolvable—issues remain. There are those, for example, who are emphatically *for* sex education for youth, *but not in the public schools*.[2] Comprehensive sex education in the public schools may not come in this generation.

As many sex education consultants can attest, discussing the need for sex education in the schools with educators and parents can be a bizarre and frustrating experience. There is seldom time enough to get into the subject in a systematic, educative manner, and the explosion of heated, emotional encounters between people who have predetermined positions often creates a situation in which a reasonable approach to the issue is impossible. Great care in the design and conduct of community sex education sessions is imperative. It is especially advantageous to all concerned if a multi-part series is offered instead of a one-evening program.

A mild case in point of the difficulty of a one-evening program is provided by a PTA meeting in an affluent New England community. Three panelists professionally involved in the field of family life and sex education were invited to address the assembled parents (a simple but unimaginative and ineffective program format). While the panelists themselves had differing emphases based on their own professional experiences, they nevertheless presented a consistent case for the incorporation of family life and sex education into the school curricula. The predominant mood of the audience, however, ranged from caution to resistance, in itself a healthy phenomenon since there is no reason why a group should passively accept the influence of reputed experts (again, the format unfortunately created an expert-layman confrontation).

Aside from the technical and valid educational issues which complicate the incorporation of education for human sexuality into the curricula, the following verbatim questions from parents illustrate the need for adult sex education.

A determined mother: "You can't teach sex without morals. I want my girls to go to me and *only* me!"

A surprised mother: "Teenagers should be taught *not* to have intimate relations because that's the best solution for everyone." She paused as she sensed an uncertain silence from those around her and then exclaimed: "Goodness, are things changing so much that this is not the right way?"

An indignant father: "Are you people going to tell the kids that it's all right to have sex urges?"

An indignant and very dignified older father: "Why do you feel parents are inadequate to teach their children [about sex]?"

The dignified wife of the dignified older father: "What about us?"

What were these parents saying (as opposed to asking), and how would you answer these questions? Take the time to think about it, perhaps with someone special, a colleague, or a small group.

## NEEDED: A SEX ETHIC FOR PLEASURE

The traditional model for "premarital" behavior is simply to behave without sex, a model which creates negative attitudes toward sex and later problems within marriage. True, the model is modified for those who intend to become married and who act responsibly toward each other by avoiding pregnancy, emotional hurts, and venereal disease. We breathe a sigh of relief when our daughters marry before the birth of the first baby. Just as long as the sequence is proper—wedding, then birth—we are even willing to ignore the fact that the bridal gown may be a maternity dress. We could consider this attitude liberal or enlightened, but in reality it is a moral cop-out, an irresponsible avoidance of the basic issue, which is that sex and marriage are now separable. What we desperately need is an ethic of sex for enjoyment and interpersonal enrichment rather than torturing the older yet prevalent ethic of sex only within marriage and for babies. If we arbitrarily project one sexual episode per week for a given man or woman from the ages of seventeen through seventy we are talking about having an experience 2,756 times, only two of which, at the most, should result in pregnancy. Yet moralistic sex education is primarily directed to those two pregnancies rather than to the purpose and lifestyle of 2,750 intimacies! It is no wonder that so much of what we consider sex education is laughed at by young adults. And it is no wonder also, that very few parents and educators are willing to face the subject honestly, for it is threatening to most of us. A sex ethic for pleasure and human growth would involve at least the following controversial aspects.

1. Consistently positive attitudes toward sexual pleasure.
2. Eradication of the double standard as harmful to both male and female sexuality.
3. Learning methods of noncoital mutual orgasm as a birth control option and as forms of enjoyable and healthy sex.

4. Availability of contraceptives from qualified agents to all who desire them.

5. Availability of medical abortions at reasonable cost, and the development of nonpunitive attitudes toward those who decide to have an abortion.

6. Knowing about surgical means for voluntary sterilization, such as vasectomy or tubal ligation.

7. Acceptance of venereal disease as a medical problem with treatment utilized and nonjudgmental attitudes toward it.

8. Availability of options for co-ed living arrangements on college campuses and wherever there are concentrations of single working people.

9. Educational methodology which values and encourages self-decision-making and the development of sensitivity and integrity.

10. Honest information about options for relational styles and modes of sexual behavior.

Which of these ten goals of education for human sexuality would you like to see adopted for society? Assuming that you are evaluating the goals for use with high-school seniors, which ones would you omit? What would you add? How would you arrange them in order of priority?

## SEX, LANGUAGE, AND HANGUPS

Adults not only have difficulty speaking about sex; they also have problems thinking about it. It's astonishing that men and women have feelings of guilt for having erotic daydreams or fantasies. But then it's not so astonishing if one remembers being chastised in school for daydreaming or assigned by the clergy to hell for "dirty thoughts." How afraid we are to use our imagination creatively and pleasurably.

The ugliness of most sex language reflects our inhibitions. We usually have only the choice between sterile technical terms or male sexist slang. Some of the "four-letter" words have powerful emotional impact and can be erotically stimulating when used in lovemaking. More often, however, they are employed to hurt or degrade others or to express anger or frustration in an explosively dramatic way. They are "bad" words because of their usual associations with bad experiences. Words in themselves are not "bad" and the significance of sex words is in the ear of the hearer. For example, one of the most obscene four-letter words can be "love." In its most profound sense "love" is shorthand for a myriad of magnificent meanings and qualities in a relationship. But it is a word that can be cruelly wielded by manipulating persons. There is more interpersonal abuse, emotional crippling, homicide, and national atrocity committed under the justification of "love" than can be described and categorized without including a vomit bag on the next page. Admittedly, this is an unusual example of the variability in meaning of "four-letter" words. But you can choose from your own examples.

The pertinent question is, can "bad" words be redeemed or is it necessary to structure a new lexicon of love? Not all sexual activity is "love," of course, but all sexual acts should be loving even when casual and on a one-experience basis. We share no common vocabulary of sex and sexuality only because we and our forebears have been too "civilized" to speak about the "unspeakable." It has been a costly silence, distorting life, deranging dreams, and inflating the power of males. The silent conspiracy of words spoken only among men is the eerie last frontier of chivalry. The secret language is a mystic medieval rite of masculinity which binds men to the code of honor: protect and shelter the virgins, "good" wives, and children from the assaults of obscenity. Translated, it means: Don't let the women know we debase them and are afraid of them, for once they understand our language of virility they will discover that we're not really big cocks but just big pricks. The liberation movement is succeeding not because women are simply becoming more bawdy, but because they have decoded sexist language and are using it with devastating results.

The full unfolding of our sexual-sensual potential in the context of joyful relationships depends in large measure on our ability to deal forthrightly with sex education for youth and with self-expression in sex language. As our attitude toward sex and sexuality changes, the semantics of sex will be in a new context. Old "dirty" words will be washed in the conversion, and the poetry of pleasuring will flourish. Certainly, the "anatomy of dirty words" is complex,[3] but whatever concerns bodily function and expression should no longer be wrapped in taboos.

We also allow our language to perpetuate fallacies about sexual functioning, thereby causing ourselves needless but painful misery and torment. Almost all adults can benefit from education about human sexual responsiveness—education which will free them from their self-designed sexual prisons. At first, it may be uncomfortable or threatening to be free. Not every insight or learning experience is pleasant. The fifty-three-year-old social worker who went through a weekend workshop on sex education was overwhelmed with amazement when he learned the facts about the clitoris; he never even knew his wife had one!—and it shook him up to wonder if he had been an inadequate lover during the thirty-five years of his marriage. In a seminar for sex educators one forty-seven-year-old male participant exclaimed with authority, "No woman can fake an orgasm!" The response of the female participants was a roar of laughter, and one woman flopped on the floor in a caricature of female climax—a spontaneous act which had everyone convulsed with hilarity. Everyone, that is, except the man who "knew" so much about women. Sex educating and counseling does have humorous episodes, but basically it is a heartbreaking responsibility to facilitate that long journey from sexual fear and ignorance to sensual liberation and joyful sexuality.

The most important part of education for human sexuality concerns human relationships. Enjoyable sex involves much more than proper techniques and good performances. Two people who care about each other share many things besides their bodies, and the quality of the sex act over a period of time reflects the quality of their relationship.

Marriage and sex counselors often see men and women who are unhappy with their sex relations because the man cannot keep an erection or the woman cannot experience an orgasm. While information about sexual techniques may be helpful in solving such problems, the difficulties are usually more complicated because of the way the partners relate to each other. All of us like instant solutions, and the successes of medical science lead us to expect simple prescriptions for fast and effective cures to medical problems. However, the inability to have and maintain an erection or to have an orgasm is rarely a medical problem; it is most often an emotional and/or relationship difficulty. It is true that the process of erections and orgasms is a natural bodily function of which almost every man and woman is capable in some degree. But as the sex researchers Masters and Johnson so clearly point out, sexual functions are unlike the other natural physical functions because they can be delayed, denied, or shaped by expectations and relationships. If a medical doctor who specializes in such problems cannot find anything wrong with the way the body and genitals function, it means that sexual difficulties have other causes. Following is a brief outline of two cases which show a connection between sexual problems and problem relationships.

*"   "   "   "   "*

Janice is a school teacher, unmarried, and thirty-three years old. For four years she has been seriously involved with Mike, a thirty-seven-year-old bachelor construction supervisor. Janice sought counseling on the insistence of Mike, who was unhappy with her apparent inability to have an orgasm. She was convinced that Mike had nothing to do with her problem because there was nothing inadequate about his sexual functioning and because he worked hard at using various techniques to bring her to orgasm. Obviously miserable because of her failure to respond to his lovemaking, Janice wanted to know what was wrong with her and what she could do to solve the problem. It was gradually clear, however, that her problem was much more complicated with the following factors:

1. When twenty-one years of age she had an abortion. Janice feels that she made the right decision but still remembers with bitterness the negative attitudes of her doctor and nurses. She already felt that she was doing something wrong according to her religion, but the medical staff made her feel more guilty and resentful by the way they judged her and treated her.

2. Her boyfriend deserted her and would not even help with the expenses of the abortion.

3. She had a negative attitude toward her own body and never masturbated because she thought it was sinful.

4. Mike takes her for granted. In the four years of dating she has restricted her interest and experience to him only. He dates other women and takes them to interesting places, yet he always sees Janice in his own apartment and never is thoughtful enough to do fun things with her by "taking her out."

5. He is always critical of her sexual "performance" and compares her unfavorably to other women.

6. Janice knows that Mike lies to her about his arrangements with other women.

7. She suspects that he really doesn't intend to marry her and actually has more resentment toward him than she will allow herself to express.

Why does Janice stay with Mike? She says that she loves him. Why is Janice unable to have an orgasm with him?

Howard has been married for almost twenty years to Susan, a conscientious housewife and mother. Both of them sought counseling because of Howard's inability to sustain an erection, a problem which began about five years earlier. Since he has not always had that difficulty he is puzzled and upset, and both he and his wife want to know how he can regain his ability to have satisfying erections.

In recent years Howard has been tense, tired, and irritable at home. Neither of them realized clearly enough that Howard had been going through a middle-age professional crisis. It is not easy for him to accept the fact that, in his mid-forties, he has reached the highest job level in his company that he will ever reach, and that his special skills are not wanted elsewhere. He is stuck where he is and feels too old to learn new job skills. He is not an easy husband to live with because he is bothered by his job situation. Although Howard and Susan are faithful to each other and see themselves as home-centered parents, Howard suspects that his wife is resentful toward him. And, as it turns out, he is correct. He is also surprised to realize his own resentments against Susan. He is an outgoing person who resents his wife's discomfort with other people. They have given up going to parties and have stopped working at developing mutual friends, and he is deeply disappointed. He has also had sexual desires that he has been afraid to express to his wife, for he senses her resistance to using hands and mouth in stimulating each other. This has been especially frustrating because for many years they practiced withdrawal before ejaculation to avoid pregnancy. Their religion did not permit the use of contraceptives.

Susan also feared pregnancy, and it was difficult for her to enjoy sexual pleasure when she had to be ready for her husband's sudden withdrawals. And she, too, had resentments. She felt that Howard was a tyrant at home and insensitive to his relationship with the three children. Although she was an attractive woman, she didn't like her own body and thought that her husband secretly wished to be married to a more beautiful woman. She also thought that sex play—using her hands and mouth to give pleasure—was somehow wrong. Susan was a sensitive person and felt that her husband appreciated her only as a wife who cooked well and kept the house clean, and as a mother who took good care of the children. She rightly wanted more, a warm friendship with Howard and a hope for the future when she could learn a new skill and work in the world outside the home. Susan was afraid that her husband would not understand her needs and that he would think of himself as a failure as a husband and a man if she sought to be more than a housekeeper and a mother.

Why do Howard and Susan stay together? They feel that they should be able to build a satisfying life together. Why does Howard have a problem with sexual response?

" " " " "

The cases of Janice and Howard show that an unsatisfying sexual relationship is based on many things. Orgasms are not automatic bodily functions; they depend on our response to the person with whom we are relating. This responsiveness depends on several important factors, explored in the next chapter.

Our sexual problems have to do with the quality of our relationships. If we realize that we influence each other's responsiveness, if we have trust, communication, intimacy, and room for personal growth, then the problem of erections or orgasms will, at best, be solvable, and at worst, be tolerable. When human relationships become more important than sex relations, we will give ourselves the best chance to allow our bodies to function naturally and to respond sexually.

# CHAPTER FOUR / INTIMACY AND SENSUAL RESPONSIVENESS

O O O O O O O O O O O O O O O O O O O O O O O O
O O O O O O O O O O O O O O O O O O O O O O O O
O O O O O O O O O O O O O O O O O O O O O O O O
O O O O O O O O O O O O O O O O O O O O O O O O
O O O O O O O O O O O O O O O O O O O O O O O O
O O O O O O O O O O O O O O O O O O O O O O O O
O O O O O O O O O O O O O O O O O O O O O O O O
O O O O O O O O O O O O O O O O O O O O O O O O
O O O O O O O O O O O O O O O O O O O O O O O O

The distorted emphasis in our society on sexual performance is fostered by such books as *The Sensuous Woman, The Sensuous Man, The Couple,* and *Any Woman Can!* It is ironic that the first three books were written by "J," "M," and "Mr. and Mrs. K," the anonymity of their names contradicting their message that sex is nothing to be ashamed about. Each of the four books does have helpful and positive aspects, and it is, of course, an injustice to lump them all together as if they were equally worthwhile or useless.[1]

The focus on lovemaking techniques and the quality and timing or orgasm neglect the other essential factors in creative intimacy which sex treatment clinics take fully into account. Such clinics or centers certainly do conduct exhaustive physiological examinations and training in sex knowledge. But they also work on the relational dynamics of a couple and educate them, through learning experiences, in sensuality awareness. Work on body image, massage, and nonverbal as well as verbal communication, is a vital part of the intensive therapeutic process. Orgasms are a result of total emotional and sensual responses. Though the rim of the penis or the head of the clitoris may provide the most intense stimulation because they are such sensitive nerve packages, these organs are connected to bodies which belong to persons. The skin, for example, is not merely a sausage casing, it is itself a sensual organ which responds to touching, rubbing, and caressing. Ashley Montagu speculates that "in the Western world it is highly probable that sexual activity, indeed the frenetic preoccupation with sex that characterizes Western culture, is in many cases not the expression of a sexual interest at all, but rather a search for the satisfaction of the need for contact."[2] It is also probable that Dr. Montagu understates the matter. Although there is certainly an extraordinary variety in the intensity of the need for contact among individuals, this need for touching and body pleasuring is at the center of sexual activity. Furthermore, the Freudian proposition that genital activity is the form of mature sex expression is an unwarranted and extreme viewpoint. The notion that the child is "polymorphically perverse" until he/she makes a transition to specific genital intercourse, is potentially harmful as a cause of needless anxieties, unrealistic expectations, and a stereotype as to what constitutes "normal" lovemaking.

People who have learned that "normal" sex means intercourse, that sensual pleasure which does not culminate in coitus is "perverse," have been misinformed and have suffered needless guilt for enjoying "unnatural" acts. Orgasms achieved through oral-genital stimulation or by mutual masturbation, for example, are not "unnatural." Rather, they are delightful methods of sex expression; acts normal, natural, and valid in themselves. The same is true for body-pleasuring experiences which do not result in orgasm for one or both partners. All lovemaking is definitely not "foreplay," for intercourse may not be the desired goal. Sex without sensuality can be a bore, and may not even be as pleasurable as masturbation, whereas sensual intimacy is usually a good experience regardless of orgastic ability or performance. Creative intimacy transcends polymorphous perversity and celebrates polymorphous sensuality.

A radical re-examination of models of sexual relationships also necessitates a repudiation of the "normalcy" of simultaneous orgasm and vaginal orgasm, notions which have been disastrous for joyful human lovemaking. Alternating orgasms—first for one partner, then for the other—can be doubly exciting and rewarding. Obviously, partners who do experience orgasm together at the same moment or a woman who climaxes while her partner's penis is within her vagina, are as "normal" as those who practice other patterns of responsiveness. The point is that not everyone does have, or should strive for, identical capacities and preferences, for there is no one model of sex expression in terms of which everyone should judge themselves (or the other) as "success" or "failure" (that's the performance bag again).

*Defining Sex Problems.* It may seem like an Alice-in-Wonderland approach to language, but there are sex problems which wouldn't be problems if we didn't think of them as sex problems. For example, premature ejaculation/orgasm, delayed ejaculation/orgasm, impotency, and frigidity. These so-called problems of sexual dysfunction are caused by Response Blocks in the self or in the relationship, but they are not medical diseases, nor are they necessarily neurotic symptoms.

There are, of course, such phenomena as "sex errors of the body"[3] and various forms of medical abnormalities and physiological dysfunctioning. There are also unusual variations of sex organ size and shape which require special understanding to cope with. There are also sex-related problems involving hormone imbalance. And it is very important to have all such medical possibilities examined by sympathetic medical specialists. It would be a step in the right direction, however, if the term "sexual dysfunction" would be used only in cases where disease, genital deformation, or organic and/or chemical causes could be demonstrated. The distinction is already being made, for example, in *primary* impotence or frigidity, as opposed to *secondary* impotence or frigidity;

medical causes involved in *primary* cases, and other causes (emotional or psychological, relational or educational) involved in *secondary* cases.

The vast majority of cases of presumed sexual dysfunction or inadequacy fall, however, in the *secondary* category, and it is questionable whether or not the term "sexual dysfunction" should be applied to all such cases. For here again, we are stuck with the Freudian model of genital activity and performance. What is premature ejaculation, for example? Is it really a matter of dysfunction? Or cannot it be simply a matter of natural male orgasm whenever the male is ready for it? If it is the latter, then perhaps the timing of ejaculation is not a question of "failure" so much as it is a question of understanding and relaxed attitudes. And what is frigidity? Is it a matter of not performing quickly enough for mutual orgasm or during intercourse? Or cannot it be a matter of natural climax whenever the female is ready and no matter how long or by what means it takes to reach that physiological-emotional state of climax? If a man and a woman are truly intimate with each other—if they enjoy the special event of their being together, and if they give themselves in total sensuality and mutual pleasuring—then it makes no difference which one comes first or even if they climax at all on a given occasion. It is sheer and senseless self-torture to worry about whether the man comes too soon or the woman doesn't come soon enough, or whether both or either climax orgastically. Masters and Johnson offer a valuable conclusion about sexual functioning. They state, "Seemingly, many cultures and certainly many religions have risen and fallen on their interpretation or misinterpretation of one basic physiological fact. Sexual functioning is a natural physiological process, yet it has a unique facility that no other physiological process, such as respiratory, bladder, or bowel function can imitate. *Sexual responsivity can be delayed indefinitely or functionally denied for a lifetime.* No other basic physiological process can claim such malleability of physical expression."[4]

The explosion of orgasm produces a momentary state of sublime unawareness of everything except intense pleasure of the self. Orgasm doesn't require intimacy with another, for obviously it can be experienced alone through masturbation and fantasy. It can also be enhanced when stimulated by another special person. But the brief inward experience fractures intimacy, which is why orgasm can result in depression or loneliness when intimacy cannot be felt following the sublime moment. And when orgasm is sought as an end in itself, it leaves a sense of desertion or debasement when no exchanges of warmth and caring follow. There are many couples who "have a lot of sex" but who suffer from sensual deprivation and a lack of intimacy.

Creative sensual intimacy with spouse and/or other friends is, then, a complex matter which involves much more than orgasms, techniques, and performances. It is also not a function of age; it is a joyous ability for a lifetime of loving. The malleability of sexual expression makes each event unique in a relationship which itself is ever-changing. Both men and women can be "frigid" in the sense that they cannot respond with relaxed warmth to their lovemaking partners. In order to create delightful events of mutual responsiveness, both men and women should be aware of the factors involved.

## Interrelated Factors in Sensual Responsiveness

There are at least eight major distinguishable factors involved in sensual responsiveness. When we have difficulty with any particular factor, we are simply having a *response block* rather than suffering from sexual dysfunction or inadequacy. Furthermore, the response block may be appropriate to our condition or relationship at any given time, *and does not necessarily indicate an emotional or relational problem.* All of these factors are interrelated in a dynamic process, and they are important for enjoyable, worthwhile intimacy whether it be heterosexual or homosexual relationships and whether the relationship is brief in duration or long-lasting.

1. *Physical Endowment.* Although the eight interrelated factors in sensual responsiveness are not listed in order of priority or importance, an obvious place to begin is with physical endowment. Perhaps it is so obvious that we miss its significance. But the simple fact is that each person is unique; different from every other person in the total combination of inherited factors, hormonal balance, body structure, and genital shape and size. Even identical twins are not totally and absolutely identical. Yet, so often, we do not accept these basic givens, and spend (waste) countless unhappy hours envying someone else's physical attributes. The dictates of fashion stimulate this envy and make us miserable when we cannot look fashionably beautiful. True, there seems to be a growing rebellion against the tyranny of fashion designers, clothing manufacturers, and cosmetic producers, but the billions of dollars still invested in the advertising media by such industries attest to our continued vulnerability. Ask yourself (and answer honestly): When was the last time you made yourself miserable by wishing some physical feature was different? Obviously, hormonal treatments, dieting, cosmetic or corrective surgery, are helpful in some cases, especially as the ageing process takes its toll. And all such medical remedies can be extremely beneficial and therapeutic. But the frantic search for stylish beauty and everlasting youthfulness is pathetic in our culture, and it requires awareness to escape being victimized by it.

Too, there is often excessive concern with genital size, especially by males. Again, the distorted emphasis on genital sex creates needless anxieties about physical adequacy. Men wonder about their "masculinity" if they feel their penis is too small (flaccid or erect); women wonder about their "femininity" if their vaginal muscles are too tight or too loose. And now that more people are aware of the essential and valuable erotic function of the clitoris, there will undoubtedly be more counseling cases with women who are anxious about the adequate size of the clitoris. Women, of course, have been forced to suffer the greatest indignity in this entire matter of physical stereotypes. As sex objects for males, they have been "educated" (brainwashed) to worry also about the size and proportions of their breasts, hips, thighs, knees, calves, ankles—actually, the entire body. Men are more obsessed with their penises than are women, however, and men are becoming subject to the same pressures of sex objectification. With the availability of nude male centerfolds in magazines, and the greater freedom of women to know intimately a variety of males, the men are beginning to be self-conscious about total body appearance. This process will require a radical readjustment of male sex attitudes if for no other reason than self-preservation. As males experience resentment and jealousy by being compared to other males, they will be starkly encountered with their own absurd attitudes and values. Ultimately, it is to be hoped that this destructive sexist game will disappear from human relationships.

Each individual can begin his/her own sexual liberation by accepting whatever body was given at the time of conception and learning to live with it.

2. *Physical Condition.* Learning to live with one's body involves making the most of what one has. Shared active experiences are more enjoyable when one has a reasonable degree of energy, endurance, and agility. And this is certainly true of lovemaking, in which breathing, motion, and strength can contribute to the pleasure of the event. Shortness of breath, muscle pain, and weakness in a basically healthy person can make times of sensual intimacy more of a trial than a time of carefree togetherness.

Do not misunderstand. This is *not* a reversion to physical stereotypes. Simply stated, no matter what anyone's body build is like, and no matter what limitations of strength and agility any person may have, some basic body care is helpful for pleasure-giving and pleasure-receiving.

Cleanliness is clearly important. It's something we undoubtedly take for granted. Yet, did our parents instruct us in the proper washing of a penis or a clitoris? (How have we instructed our children?) Are we aware of dirty or ragged fingernails and/or toenails? What does it taste like when you put your tongue into an earful of wax? Little things to be sure, and some of them humorous. And yet little things can be distracting enough to turn us off. Pimples, sweat, and odors are a natural part of the human body, and there is such a thing as obsessive cleanliness. Sexual contact itself is not "dirty," but it can also be more delightful when it's with someone who is not careless about cleanliness.

Exercise, in some modest degree, can be beneficial to muscle tone and physical endurance, and a contribution to sensuous well-being as well as to general health. Even a large and heavy person can move with greater gracefulness if he/she develops the strength necessary to move with ease. For various reasons, most people cannot become versatile sexual athletes, especially in terms of assuming a large variety of intercourse postures. The one thousand and one positions shown in picture books should be looked upon as visual erotic entertainment rather than as a guidebook. For most of us just do not have such bendable bodies. It is also one thing for a male simply to pose in those positions; it is another for him to maintain an erection in all those positions. It is also not the case that all couples are perfectly matched in size, strength, and sexual ability. But even in the richer variety of sensual pleasuring, some strength in hands, back, stomach, and legs—even jaw and tongue—is essential. (O.K.—visualize a person sitting at a desk and wiggling his/her tongue. Certainly a funny sight, but hardly a stupid exercise.) To give a massage, for example, requires conditioning of many muscles, especially when a table of the proper height is not available (besides which, it's more pleasurable on a bed or on the floor).

A consideration of the physical condition factor by any individual should also require an examination of the use of drugs, alcohol, and cigarettes as they relate to sensual awareness. While each person will be guided by personal experience and medical advice, it is well to reflect upon the fact that anything which dulls the responses of the senses impedes ability to be sensuously alive. Smoking, drinking, and the taking of some drugs may provide relaxation and temporary freedom from inhibitions for some people. But taken in excessive amounts (which vary from person to person) they can react as sensory depressants. An individual may desire or need these experiences for many reasons, but should not be surprised when they interfere with or block sensual responsiveness. In any case, the use of such materials should be examined by any person exploring his/her response blocks.


3. *Emotional State and Communication.* There are times when we are not present in a shared reality; times when we can be locked in private meditation, frustration, anxiety—and a host of emotional states. Our moods vary, sexual interest and need levels change, depression or tiredness can plague us, and fantasy can envelop us. We're not always *present* with and for our partner. And why should we expect otherwise? Because of romantic notions of constant togetherness? Because of a need to have constant approval from the other? Differences in emotional states at a given time can shatter intimacy if the couple operate with unrealistic expectations of simultaneous feelings, interests, and needs. It is a denial of the autonomy and personhood of the other which eventually leads to deep discord.

Anger over unresolved issues or conflicts can also lead to temporary alienation. It is also an opportunity to create a richer and more profound intimacy if it is communicated with sensitivity and imagination. But while a person is actually feeling angry, it will be impossible to respond to a partner who does not perceive that anger. And that's when the anger is often expressed with destructive hostility. One of the sex stereotype fallacies is that it is typical of the female to deny closeness when she is angry. And the typical male response is supposed to be exasperation with the mercurial moods of mysterious womanhood. This indeed does happen, but it is a pathetic male defensiveness in the face of his own shallowness. Or the response can be insultingly patronizing: "Honey, you sure look sexy when you're mad." At such times a male may pursue sex contact and subconsciously or deliberately use his penis as a thrusting weapon, smugly congratulating himself for his "virility." That kind of sex is dehumanizing, and certainly without intimacy. Fortunately, males cannot be stereotyped either, for there are countless numbers of them who are sensitive and who share similar human responses with females. A man can also experience a response block when he is angry or upset, and this kind of response block in both men and women is *not* a symptom of neurosis, sexual dysfunctioning, or inadequacy. Since so many women have, subconsciously and consciously, justifiable grievances against their male partners, it is understandable that large numbers of them should be sexually and sensually unresponsive to some extent.

People who are involved in valued work invest psychic energy and emotion in the work, and may, for varying periods, be so preoccupied with it, that sensual intimacy will temporarily have a lower priority in their living. In our orgasm-counting culture, it may be an embarrassment to report a low sex outlet incidence for any given period, the assumption being that higher frequencies of orgasm are supposed to be more normal, or in some way healthier. Such an assumption is ridiculous. It ignores individuality, the quality of an orgasmic experience, the preference for nonorgasmic intimacy, and the nonsexual values of a full life. In any case, it will be more difficult for spouses to find or create times for physical and emotional closeness when both of them have demanding and meaningful work. Work, of course, can be an escape from a relationship; an excuse for avoiding contact. But when long hours are eagerly anticipated, and when work is pursued with singlemindedness, the resulting state of preoccupation should not be interpreted as rejection. Goals accomplished stimulate personal growth, which in turn allows more complete persons to have joy in and with each other.

Another influence on our emotional state which causes response blocks, is negative *attitudes* about sex. It bears mention in this context for the simple reason that feelings of shame, disgust, or fear toward the body or the genitals, prevents a *total* response of the self to the special other. Although sensual awareness and responsiveness involve more than coital activity, it is a depth of intimacy which can be blocked by rejection of, or discomfort with, any part of the body. To be anointed by loving touch of hand or mouth on any point of yearning flesh, and yet to freeze and withhold response, is to refuse a gift of human grace which infuses life with happiness. And to be unable to offer the same gift is doubly sad.

The full range of interpersonal intimacy encompasses more than exchanges in bodily pleasuring. And response blocks caused by emotional states need not be insurmountable for those who work at mutual understanding. This requires the use of reason and honest conversation. The communion of sensual intimacy is rarely sustained without the intimacy of verbal communication. Talk, self-expression in words, is critically important for a worthwhile relationship. People who have nothing to say to each other, or who are afraid of revealing themselves through speech, are not going to be able to sustain the celebrative dimensions of physical contact. To be sure, the nonverbal communication of body language and behavior must reinforce words. And words are always inadequate to express the full meaning of feelings and experiences. Nevertheless, language is an art which enriches humanness immeasurably. To know someone intimately is to share their being in past experience, present aliveness, and future potentiality. Only words can convey these dimensions of the self and the other. There are times when conversational sharing of intensely personal feelings and thoughts can create an exhilarating intimacy, achievable in no other way. Self-revelation through verbal expression can, of course, be risky. It is not easy to risk rejection or ridicule. And negative feelings and attitudes are always difficult to verbalize in a helpful way. But not to choose those risks is to risk the deterioration of a relationship and the emotional death of the self.

4. *Environment and Time.* Erotic enjoyment can be hindered or enhanced by environmental influences and the time available for relaxation and response. Eleven o'clock at night, between the sheets, with the lights out; this is the setting for sexual tragedy. Not that there's anything wrong with eleven o'clock, or darkness, or beds, but when this combination becomes routine to the exclusion of other possibilities, sexual activity becomes boring if not burdensome, and sleep is the welcome reliever. It is understandable that during the work week, early morning and bedtime are the only available times for most couples. But lovemaking needn't be unimaginatively restricted to those automatic bedroom hours. Although spontaneity in mutual pleasuring is a delightful occurrence (including the passionate kiss in the kitchen or the erotic shower in the bathroom) it is possible and advantageous to *plan* sensual sessions. A holiday or a weekend can provide great expectations when the event is planned by having other members of the household absent for at least a few hours. Then a silenced phone, a bottle of wine, dancing candlelight, sensuous music, pillows by the fireplace, and a favorite body lotion, become ingredients for a memorable experience. Such an event may not be possible to arrange often, but its happening requires forethought and a kind of planned spontaneity. Within the special time of privacy together, inhibition dissolves, and laughter and joy attend the naked frolic.

The location of a bedroom can also be an inhibiting influence, especially in small houses. Sounds and motion play a vital part in zestful pleasuring. If children or in-laws inhabit adjacent bedrooms, most people feel self-conscious about their lovemaking sounds, language, and movements. This can be a difficult situation to resolve, but the best attitude to assume is, "If family and friends can hear us argue, we owe it to them to let them hear us loving."

The concern over environmental and time factors does not require perfect conditions for lovemaking sessions. Brief petting or quickie orgasms provide a delightful change of pace and variety in erotic relationships. Any one ritualized way of "doing it" becomes as boring or ridiculous as the phrase itself. The point is simply that we are not often enough aware of the inhibiting influences of hurried encounters in unsatisfying places. And we can do something about this source of response blocks through awareness and planning.

5. *Appreciation of Partner.* In the long run, the ability to respond totally is blocked if there is no appreciation of, and respect for, the spouse or other partner. The quality of the relationship matters. Without friendship based on some shared values and mutual likability, sensual intimacy becomes impossible. It is amazing how some people expect themselves to be sensuously alive with partners they don't even like. It's easier for friends to become lovers than for lovers to become friends. A couple starting out with an intense level of physical involvement can't always make the transition to a friendship relationship. Which is one of the reasons why monogamous alliances are difficult to sustain. Mutual appreciation in friendship is indispensable for intimacy. Without this spiritual dimension of intimacy, all kinds of emotional response blocks develop, including self-hate.

Appreciating the *beingness* of a particular friend is an experience which needs such words as "spiritual" or "religious" for description. Something happens in the exchange of affection and affirmation which transforms the relationship into something greater than the sum of its parts. A marriage without this celebrative in-touchness with life becomes merely an exercise in dutiful role-playing. An intriguing question which often is asked during discussions of this fifth factor in sensual responsiveness relates to the significance of so-called casual sex. What about the one-night or weekend sexual encounter with a stranger(s)? Should this be any less enjoyable or satisfying simply because there hasn't been time for the development of communication and mutual appreciation? Coming to terms with such questions is especially urgent for single, divorced, or widowed individuals who meet others briefly and have to make quick decisions. Obviously, each person will have to evaluate his/her situation and risk a personal conclusion. "Casual" sex with a stranger can be unpleasant, humiliating, and even dangerous (e.g., V.D. or emotionally unstable behavior). But it can be a positive experience for people who know themselves fairly well, who are perceptive in evaluating the personality and intentions of others, and who explore mutual expectations *verbally* (even if briefly). It seems as if there are ever-increasing numbers of people who are being sensitized to tenderness, caring, and understanding; people who also have few sexual hangups and a strong need for physical, sensual closeness. Such people can often recognize each other within minutes. When the "vibes" are right, further nonverbal explorations take place. The "casual" relationship can be quite heavy. And it can be a memorable and liberating experience.

6. *Attractiveness of Partner.* What we see in another person is more than what we see with our eyes. We see with experience, memory, lust, esthetic values, and personal needs and desires. Have you ever looked at a couple and wondered to yourself what they could possibly see in each other?

Attractiveness involves physical endowment and condition plus something more: personality and character. Because of various subtle and subconscious elements involved in inter-personal dynamics, a particular person may turn you on but leave someone else cold. This is one of the practical problems of open-ended marital pairing: two couples do not always make it as a foursome. In any case, mutual attraction is a unifying force between two people who delight in each other's presence. Indeed, just thinking of each other can provide quiet happiness.

Attractiveness has more to do with self-image than body-image, and nothing to do with the stereotypic models of Mr. and Ms. America. The eyes that reflect alertness and interest; the voice which conveys gentle self-confidence; the hands which touch with caring grace—such are the marks of attractiveness.

7. *Self-Esteem.* "Why is it that so many of us do not like ourselves?" This is a question asked over and over again by participants in seminars, conferences, and workshops. It is a question asked with a mixture of regret and resentment. The question is a critical one. If we do not like ourselves, why should we expect someone else to like us? Indeed, we are often surprised at—and suspicious of—someone who likes us with more intensity than we feel we deserve. We can even contrive, subconsciously, to make people dislike us, thus validating our negative self-image.

It is not easy to regard oneself with respect and admiration, as having high value. There is a thin line between self-esteem and selfish, arrogant pride on the one side, and self-effacing humility on the other. Rather than risk finding our center—our wholeness—because of possible rejection and ridicule, we underestimate ourselves. Having self-esteem does not mean invulnerability to hurt. But it does require a ground or center of being strong enough to continue risk-taking *in spite of the hurts.* To have self-esteem is to integrate negative past experiences—especially shame and humiliation—and to sense with dignity one's abilities and potentialities. Self-esteem is the ability to forgive one's self and to seek new dimensions of personal growth without fear. With self-esteem, communication is more honest and behavior less inhibited. The woman or man with self-esteem is an authentic person rather than an actor with many masks.

This quality of self-affirmation enriches sensual responsiveness by allowing the individual to *receive* pleasure and to take initiative and responsibility for his/her own orgasms. It creates an attitude which conveys the message: "Yes, I am worthy of your loving attention and do accept your pleasuring gladly and appreciatively. And when I feel the need for orgasm, I will receive your sensuous gifts with joy and without shame."

8. *Sex Knowledge.* Anyone who knows everything he/she always wanted to know about sex has a very limited capacity for knowledge. And anyone who has imagination, creativity, and cares about human relations will always dare to ask questions. For there will always be much to wonder about and discover when it comes to human sexuality with all its bodily mysteries and varieties of expression.

All of the factors in sensual responsiveness involve sex knowledge, of course. Yet, continued learning is important in order that one may *give* pleasure in lovemaking. It is always encouraging to see people well over the age of sixty attending sex education sessions because such education is valuable throughout the life cycle. It's not just kid stuff. And persons who choose to become involved in open-ended sensual intimacy will find that every partner is a new chapter in educational experience. The general principles of sex information cannot be applied in precisely the same way with different persons and relationships; learning must take place with each partner.

There are learning limitations to marriage manuals, textbooks, and erotic visual materials, especially with regard to their undervaluing of nonintercourse sensuality and intimacy; the sensual intimacy which transcends orgasm and which can be happily enjoyed throughout life.[5] Nevertheless, it is certainly worthwhile to be knowledgeable about continued advances in sex research and effective methods for sensual pleasuring, especially when such information is *shared* with a caring partner.

## SUGGESTIONS FOR USING THE IFSR INVENTORY

Individuals who feel that they do have Response Blocks which prevent satisfying sensual responsiveness might clarify their condition or situation by taking the time to reflect upon the eight interrelated factors previously described. Make a list:

*A    B*

\_\_  \_\_  physical endowment
\_\_  \_\_  physical condition
\_\_  \_\_  emotional state and communication
\_\_  \_\_  environment and time
\_\_  \_\_  appreciation of partner
\_\_  \_\_  attractiveness of partner
\_\_  \_\_  self-esteem
\_\_  \_\_  sex knowledge

In column A, rank all eight factors in order of most difficulty or trouble for you; in other words, number one would be the factor which most bothers you and number eight would be placed beside the factor which least bothers you. Refer to the descriptions of each factor to refresh your memory and stimulate your thinking.

After column A is completed, move to column B and again rank order the factors, but this time do it on the basis of how you think your partner would rank the factors for himself/herself.

If your partner also does the exercise and you are both willing to risk sharing lists with each other for the sake of deeper communication, then do it in two stages. First, each of you explain to the other why you chose the first three factors for yourselves. Secondly, check your perceptions of each other by comparing what you thought the partner would choose for the first three to what was actually chosen. Whether the inventory is checked alone or used with a partner, however, the important point is to *do* something to improve the factors which most bother you. Even a change of attitude or a painfully honest conversation may make a critical difference in your ability to value and enjoy your own body and someone else's.

# CHAPTER FIVE / VARIETIES OF ALTERNATIVE LIFESTYLES AND MODES OF SEXUAL BEHAVIOR

O O O O O O O O O O O O O O O O O O O O O O O O O
O O O O O O O O O O O O O O O O O O O O O O O O
O O O O O O O O O O O O O O O O O O O O O O O O O
O O O O O O O O O O O O O O O O O O O O O O O O O
O O O O O O O O O O O O O O O O O O O O O O O O O
O O O O O O O O O O O O O O O O O O O O O O O O
O O O O O O O O O O O O O O O O O O O O O O O O O
O O O O O O O O O O O O O O O O O O O O O O O O
O O O O O O O O O O O O O O O O O O O O O O O O O

In spite of the tensions and controversies surrounding the issues of human sexuality in the United States, this country is witnessing a proliferation of alternative lifestyles. It is not that any particular lifestyle is historically new, for precedents can be found for every one of the relational patterns which constitute a lifestyle. What is relatively new, however, is that people can make choices about the nontraditional ways in which they wish to live; choices made with awareness and without the burden of shame or irrational guilt.

The term "lifestyle" is, of course, ambiguous. It lacks clear definition and is used in a variety of ways, especially when it refers to activities or interests or roles which are central to a person's life. An olympic or professional athlete, for example, does not merely participate in a sport. Rather, that sport becomes a focus around which the athlete organizes his/her living. As such, one can have a lifestyle of an athlete; or a politician; or a clergyman; or a housewife; or a scholar. And on and on. But a word which can be used in so many different ways becomes jargon and soon loses its meaning.

As used in this book, however, lifestyle refers to *relational patterns* between people: the way in which individuals organize their lives in relationship to others. These lifestyles are "alternative" primarily to the traditional monogamous marriage and the nuclear family—one husband and one wife and their children. Furthermore, alternative lifestyles require awareness and choice on the part of the person or persons involved. A criminal in prison, for example, might be described as a person living in a same sex community. There are very few prisoners, however, who choose incarceration as a lifestyle. The same may be said of a reluctant draftee although, of course, there are significant differences between prison cells and military bases. Or take the example of a teenager or unmarried woman who unintentionally becomes pregnant and gives birth because of the unavailability of other options in terminating an unwanted pregnancy. It happens a few hundred thousand times each year. Such predicaments would not be considered alternative lifestyles, although, as we shall see, the choice to nurture the child rather than to have it adopted does make a difference: the difference between being an unwed mother or a single parent.

There is no scholarly consensus on the number of alternative lifestyles, and, though the number is limited, it will probably never be fixed with precision because of the various possible combinations and the continual inventiveness of human beings. There is also no sure statistical count of the numbers of persons experimenting with nontraditional relational patterns and we can expect numerous studies and surveys to contribute to our understanding as to what is really happening in contemporary society. Some innovations seem to be taking place on a large scale, and some are little more than ideas or theories. In any case, what is significant is the relentless challenge to the traditional model of monogamous marriage with all of its attendant role stereotypes and behavioral expectations. In order to gain some perspective on the changing marital and familial scene, let us hazard a brief description of twelve varieties of alternative lifestyles.

1. *Traditional Monogamy.* It is ironic, and perhaps unobvious, that the various alternatives to traditional monogamy have, in turn, made this common lifestyle optional. The culturally programmed progression from parent-child separation through temporary single.ood and advanced education to marriage and parenthood is no longer *the* model for adulthood. It is simply one among many models, and, as such, deserves careful reconsideration. For it is, after all, the major model for the vast majority of men and women. It merits improvement rather than snide condemnation. And those who choose it should be better prepared to cope creatively with the terms of the contract. Traditional monogamy is marriage which is intended to last as long as both partners live. Even in the increasing instances where couples change the traditional wedding vows to "as long as love shall last" from "as long as we both shall live," the sincere hope is that their love will ever deepen and grow. It is rare for people to marry with the carefree attitude of: "What the hell, if it doesn't work out we can always get divorced." True enough, attitudes and intentions often change after the wedding. But nobody likes to make the solemn commitment of marriage without believing and feeling that life is going to be more beautiful for each because of their loving union. Indeed the outward forms and the words of the wedding ceremony are being conscientiously experimented with precisely because young people today are determined to begin their marriages with joyful and honest celebration. Their hopes for love, dreams of happiness, and desires for the fullness of life are universal even though expressed in untraditional ways.

Traditional marriage is characterized by monogamy—one husband with one wife, and sexual fidelity—the exclusion of all others from the intimacy of lovemaking. Although this lifestyle is cheapened by the double standard and mocked by the high rate of failure in divorce, its most serious threat comes from the incredible weight of functions it must serve. Modern marriage is almost a disaster because of the beguiling attractiveness of its many layers. Husband, wife, and kids stand on frosted tiers of unrealistic expectations and it shouldn't be surprising that so many family constructions eventually crumble. We expect too much of ourselves, of each other, and of the fragile complexity of marital and family relationships. To be all things to each other at all times under all circumstances is to be defeated.

But those who prophesy the death of the traditional marriage and family are shortsighted. Human beings *do* learn from experience. And there is every justification for devising enlightened educational programs to train people to cope creatively with the values and ideals of monogamous, sexually exclusive wedlock. Since it is, and will continue to be, the preferred lifestyle of millions, all of us have a stake in helping it work and achieve its goals. Admittedly, the task is formidable, formidable because it requires hard self-appraisals and courageous communication. A good beginning is the realization—and acceptance of the fact—that marriage is not a solution to living but a step in life. A risky step. While recognizing its lofty and lovely aims, it is necessary to divest it of romantic crap. A good beginning is the adoption of realistic and honest curricula in family living and education for human sexuality in junior and senior high schools across the country. It is pathetic that those who scream loudest about the deterioration of marriage and family life in America tend to be those who vociferously oppose good education in these fields for young people. A renewal and reshaping of traditional marriage is impossible without a rededication and resensitizing to humanizing education for all ages. *All* ages. Let us share with young people the human pains, frustrations, agonies, and puzzles of married life. Let us trust them to feel the magnificence of loving and living without pretending that crises and tragedies will not be a part of their loving and living. Let us help them with their self-esteem and confidence by supporting them in their intentions to be sexually faithful to each other without pretending that openness and affection toward others is a betrayal of faithfulness. Traditional marriage can be open and creative if we will but give it growing room in our society. Because it is *chosen*, it has a higher value rather than being something to be endured.

2. *Child-free Marriage.* "Married six years and no children? . . . Oh, I'm sorry, I shouldn't have asked. . . . But have you thought of adopting?" Yes, the pressure is bad enough for married couples who cannot have children for medical reasons. The irrational sense of inadequacy and failure can sometimes be emotionally destructive. Imagine, then, the pressure on couples who remain childless by choice; relentless pressure from parents whose "right" to grandparenthood has been betrayed; from married friends who have assumed the burden of parenthood and resent the freedom and financial comfort of the child-free couple. "Selfish!" The message is clear to the child-free spouses: "Feel guilty!" It's a different matter, of course, if the childlessness is simply a tragedy—pity can be felt for the poor man and wife who can never know the joy and privilege of creating a new life, flesh of their flesh, bone of their bones. But to have this ability and deliberately reject parenthood is to threaten others. It's abnormal. It's blasphemous.

Negative reactions to the married child-free are understandable if not justified. Marriage and parenthood are synonymous. The child-free couple continuously face the question: "If you didn't want to have any kids, what the hell did you get married for in the first place?"—a question that reveals much about the quality of the questioners' marriage. Even the parents of a child-free couple are pressured to feel guilty. "So, when's your Sally going to present you with a grandson? What's wrong with those two?" Naturally, the emphasis is usually on the male line of genealogical immortality. The snide and cutting remarks can be quite subtle and imaginative, but their impact is felt. And it can hurt.

Fortunately, the child-free advocates are stating their case for the validity of their lifestyle. In a world where overpopulation is a problem, they need feel no guilt for refusing to procreate. On the contrary, they can feel positive about not adding to the problem. Though it is not easy to cope with the envy of others, it is becoming easier to live well without apology or feelings of selfishness. Isn't everybody searching for a measure of material comfort and personal happiness? And even if there is no dramatic singleminded career of social service to rationalize the rejection of parenthood, there is satisfaction in contributing to the reappraisal of the purposes and motives of creating children. Not all men and women *should* become fathers and mothers; not all babies enrich the marital relationship. There are good reasons to believe that the human race would live in a happier place if all babies born were wanted and were nurtured by able men and women who enjoyed the art of parenting.

The child-free couple do face challenges to the marriage, challenges which are typical of all marriages. And they cannot as easily hide their relational problems by concentrating on the needs and problems of children. Nevertheless, if they can find paths to personal growth and interpersonal enjoyment, they are usually years ahead of those parents who do not begin to become persons until the children have left home.

3. *Single Parenthood.* Unplanned pregnancies and so-called "illegitimate" births are hardly a new social phenomenon. It's as old as intercourse and marriage contracts. What is new is a daring attitude of female independence and decision-making which values parenthood without benefit of marriage. Whether the pregnancy is intentional or not, marriage simply for the sake of providing a legal father is rejected as hypocrisy. In the few publicized cases of celebrities with ample financial resources, single motherhood is admired as a courageous protest against tradition. But in the more typical cases of financial hardship, where public aid to families with dependent children is involved, a harsher public judgment is applied. In any case, something new is happening. In more recent times, an unwanted pregnancy was resolved either by abortion

or adoption. But now there are much more tolerant and understanding attitudes toward single mothers who choose—sometimes with the support of parents and friends—to raise the child without the benefit of father or matrimony. Special schools for pregnant teenagers are being formed and even in the public schools pregnant girls have won constitutional rights to equal education and are being treated more humanely. Single men and women are also winning the right to be adoptive parents. What this phenomenon means is not yet clear. It is probably a transitional phase toward universal planned parenthood. In the meantime, it is certain that unintentional pregnancies will decreasingly force females into shameful hiding. Sex is natural for both sexes, and males will have to share the price for the maintenance of sexual ignorance and irresponsibility.

4. *Singlehood.* The literature on human behavior regularly refers to "premarital" development and experiences on the assumption that nearly all men and women intend to marry. There are, of course, the poor unfortunates who apparently don't have what it takes to catch a spouse, but these, along with lesbians and homosexuals, are unusual exceptions to the human destiny of marital union. The adult who is not single by choice can be miserably unhappy, especially when confronted by the nagging inquiries of parents and relatives. Even when a person does remain single by choice, he/she often faces leering suspicions of sexual queerness. However, the opposite supposition could as easily be made, namely, that single adults are more intelligent and emotionally healthy than wedded adults since they have avoided the probabilities of marital misery. The more reasonable attitude should be approval of those who have the sense to explore life and people before making that awesome commitment to one other person. After all, even if one marries for mature companionship in his/her forties, there is still the possibility of a good thirty-year

marriage. The trend away from teenage marriage indicates that greater numbers of young adults are valuing their state of singlehood prior to "settling down."

But why "settle down" at all? It's certainly not necessary for an interesting and worthwhile professional career. Not in this mobile society. Yet it is the mobility of single people which is envied, and we resent seeing people enjoy themselves without family responsibilities. A single person does, however, have economic and psychological problems to contend with: The high cost of urban living and the periods of loneliness, which can be depressing. Most single people do not enjoy living alone.

Perhaps young people should be trained for singlehood; e.g., women learning car maintenance and repair, and men learning how to cook and maintain and repair clothing. Some high schools do offer such learning opportunities, and the enthusiasm of the participants proves that sex-role stereotypes are indeed being demolished.

5. *Communes.* The need and desire to share resources and experiences with others provide the underlying motivation for communal living. There are undoubtedly thousands of communal-type units in the United States, but how many nobody knows. Certainly, if we include shared apartments as mini-communes, the number would be in the hundreds of thousands. In every urban and university center there are countless students sharing space, rent, food costs and preparation, housecleaning duties, and recreational activities. This arrangement alleviates both financial hardship and loneliness.

The classification of communes would in itself require an entire book. There are short-term and long-term units. Common interests may be professional, craft, agrarian, philosophical, political, therapeutic, religious, or some combination thereof. The number of participants varies, and the members may be single, married, divorced, or widowed. Children and all ages are involved. Communes are located in urban, rural, and suburban regions. Some are highly structured while others are anarchistic. Some allow the retention of private wealth and others require the total pooling of all resources from each member. The patterns of sexual relationships also vary from puritanical to permissive, from monogamy to multirelational openness. It should be obvious, then, that the concept of commune covers a multitude of phenomena.

Communes sometimes belong to cooperatives with other communes, often to increase their purchasing power. There are associations to introduce neophytes to the communal lifestyle and to get potential communards in contact with each other. There is even a national open-ended community which offers the availability of its members as facilitators in communal organization. It is, indeed, a substantial movement in contemporary society.

Members of communes invariably discover the experience to be a challenge to self-growth. Those who cannot cope drop out, while others struggle to satisfy needs for privacy and intimacy. It is not an easy task.

6. *Cohabitation.* Cohabitation refers to two people living together without matrimonial sanction. The practice is neither novel nor rare. In some states it is legally sanctioned through statutes recognizing common law marriage. Some couples consider themselves morally married but for financial, legal, or ideological reasons ignore the technicality of civil or religious matrimony. Some divorced people refuse to rush into remarriage and simply live together for mutual affection, companionship, and financial support. In many cases the woman's self-esteem depends on working and having financial independence. Thus, she does not feel like a "kept woman" and also has the internal resources to ignore gossip from nosy neighbors: "The hell with them—nobody owns me." Even elderly, retired men and women are known to live together without marriage, especially when their social security payments are reduced because of a change in marital status.

Trial marriage has also been a controversial topic for discussion for the past fifty years. Trial marriage is, of course, not marriage technically, for we do not yet have legal two-degree or multi-stage marriage license procedures, though that practice will someday be institutionalized.

Cohabitation as an alternative lifestyle has, in the last few years, surged into the open among counterculture college-age young people. Workers and students advertise frankly in the underground press for someone to share life without promises of marriage. College students in coed dormitories manage, for all practical purposes, to live with their lovers. And off-campus cohabitation is casually accepted whereas a few years ago it was still scandalous and condemned. Since universities no longer assume the rights of parental authority, and since eighteen-year-olds are increasingly being granted the civil rights of adulthood, it is likely that the trend of young couples living with each other will continue. This doesn't mean, of course, that most parents are enthusiastic about such living arrangements, or that society bestows its approval. It doesn't even mean that all students participating in such experiments are going to benefit from the experience. But it does mean that sex education and health services related to young adults will have to be more realistic and effective.

7. *Second-Chance Monogamy.* While the subject of divorce merits more prolonged consideration than is appropriate in this section, it is important to include the widespread phenomenon of marital dissolution and remarriage in a discussion of alternative lifestyles. Certainly, and unhappily, not all divorces are obtained with awareness and choice on the part of the parties. The majority of divorces—and not necessarily only contested cases—involve confusion and unsatisfactory compromise on the part of at least one partner. Nevertheless, divorce is an institutionalized form of second-chance monogamy, and with more humane and rational laws governing the legal dissolution of marriage, more couples are choosing this

step toward the renewal of their lives. While some divorced persons will engage in other lifestyles, such as cohabitation or communes, it appears that most will seek remarriage. With hopes of being wiser and more mature, they will nevertheless seek that one other special person with whom to establish a traditional marriage. If children were part of the picture, it will not be possible for either ex-partner to return to singlehood even though many try to play that game. The realities of being a parent, no matter which one has custody of the children, will always remain to some degree. If, however, no children were born, and if the personal sense of failure can be overcome, and if one can ignore the still existing social stigmata upon the divorced, and if one is still young enough, it is possible to resume the lifestyle of singlehood. And, of course, the task is made more difficult for women than it is for men.

The vindictive, absurd, and archaic divorce laws still common in this country must eventually be radically reformed to allow human beings to grow beyond past choices for the sake of new hope and new possibilities of self-fulfillment.

8. *Swinging and Group Sex.* In fantasy, possibly ninety-nine percent of wives and husbands have wished for, or been curious about, sexual and sensual experiences with someone other than their spouses. For a small but growing number of married persons, fantasy has become reality. And few of these people are members of the Sexual Freedom League or Flower Children. They include middle-aged, middle-class men and women who otherwise lead conventional lives.

Swingers are married or unmarried couples who together meet other couples with the intention of pairing off with each other for sexual pleasuring. The old-fashioned term used to be "wife-swapping" but the obvious sexist indignity of that term was changed to "mate-swapping" or "spouse-swapping." And the mechanical, impersonal implications of those terms were replaced with the more carefree and equalitarian term "swinging." While swingers are still discreet about their behavior, especially to "straight" acquaintances, they consider their activities as a healthful recreational pastime rather than as indulgence in perversion, vice, or sin.

Though a few studies of swingers have been published, it is presumptuous to stereotype such participants of this lifestyle. Some couples enjoy the impersonal nature of such encounters—impersonal in the sense that they expect of each other no emotional attachment. Other couples delight in nurturing friendship and knowing others more intimately. And not all swingers participate in group sex; while they may enjoy looking and being looked at, they pair off rather than have three or more in a group experience. There are, of course, many other differences between swingers and swinging styles. Anyone who needs to be convinced of the phenomenon simply needs to read the ads for threesomes, foursomes, and groups in the underground press (some of which are quite aboveground).

Whatever risks and benefits swinging might provide for its participants, it is a clear challenge to the myth that marriage cannot survive without sexual exclusiveness.

9. *Family Networks.* Family networks may be defined as voluntary extended families, though they are not families in a blood-line sense. Family networks provide a type of open-ended community, and they are not necessarily confined to geographical proximity. One such network, for example, is comprised of a dozen classmates who went to graduate school together. They and their spouses have been camping together every summer for almost twenty years and the children consider that they have numerous "cousins, aunts, and uncles." The adults deeply care for each other and each other's children. They have contingency funds to help each other financially and they intervene therapeutically in each other's personal, professional, and family crises. They have maintained sexual fidelity to their spouses, but are open, in recent years, to other alternatives. They are what can be called a community-in-dispersion.

Another example of a family network involves several families who do live in the same town. They are similar in economic and professional achievement. Weekends, holidays, vacations, are often shared, and there is a degree of discipline in their structure. Retreats and encounter sessions keep them tuned to each other and sexual lovemaking is not restricted to spouses.

The elements of the family network are, of course, not new. They have been traditionally embodied in close-knit neighborhoods, especially those which were bonded by ethnic and religious values, and intermarital ties. There are also many quasi-family networks which are informal associations of three or four couples. These people feel like family to each other and are, in fact, often closer friends than are relatives. They do such things as barbecue together, party together, borrow from each other, help each other with home repairs, and take care of each other's kids.

Family network members are, however, more conscious of their relationships and common goals or interests. They are aware of their responsibilities toward each other and work at communication and community. Family networks chart a middle course between communes and group marriage.

10. *Group Marriage.* Anyone who has experienced the trials of traditional marriage must surely laugh at the advocates of group marriage. "It's bad enough to make a go of it with one spouse ... how can anybody enjoy living with two or more spouses?" Well, one can imagine a myriad of earthy reactions to any proposal for group marriage.

Legally, there is no such thing as group marriage. Our society recognizes only one form of marriage: heterosexual monogamy. True, there is a compromise with divorce, but divorce serves the purposes of monogamy in that it supports a system of one spouse at a time. The Mormons must be startled, bemused, or indignant by the practice of group marriage. They, of course, were unconstitutionally forced to abandon the lifestyle of polygamy which was based on their religious beliefs and values. Although the practice has not been eradicated, it is ironic that the society which suppressed their conscientious familial pattern now permits without legal sanction experiments in group marriage. It is possible and would not be surprising if strong social forces of reaction moved to prosecute all those who are tampering with the sacred tradition of heterosexual monogamy. Society is trying to digest a large number of basic and rapid changes, and periodic reactionary vomiting can be expected, one of the last upsurges being the crusade against sex education in public schools. The pioneers of social change forge on, however, and those engaged in group marriage are exploring unfamiliar familial territory.

Group marriage is neither polygamous nor polyandrous by definition. There *may* be one husband with co-wives, or one wife with co-husbands. But there also might be multiple wives with multiple husbands in a variety of combinations. It is the intentional and commitment factors which differentiate group marriages from communes, though sometimes the difference can be imperceptible. The partners in a group marriage make a moral commitment to each other, a commitment which involves love, support, the intention to remain together, and all of the responsibilities of traditional marriage. The spouses might also be sexually exclusive in the sense that sexual intimacy is reserved only for the marriage partners. Or the group marriage may be open-ended, with each spouse free to enjoy sexual experience with friends outside the marriage. Needless to say, it is critical for the terms of the marriage contract to be clear and understood by each spouse.

Researchers Larry Constantine and Joan Constantine tell us about the whys and wherefores of group marriage in their impressive studies and publications.[1]

11. *Synergamous Marriage.* Synergamous marriage is not only difficult to pronounce, it's difficult to imagine. But leave it to the creative imagination of Robert Rimmer to produce

a novel, *Thursday, My Love,* around the concept.[2] Essentially, synergamous marriage is akin to bigamy or trigamy, or possibly, double bigamy or triple trigamy. *Thursday, My Love,* concerns a case of double bigamy. Adam, the man, has a wife and family but also marries Angela, who has a husband and family. Adam and Angela know that each has a legal spouse, and, though they love their spouses and value their marriages, they also love each other. So much so, that they become morally married in a religious ceremony performed by a daring futuristic Jesuit. With skill and ingenuity, Adam and Angela arrange their lives to spend part of every week with each other in their love-nest apartment in, of all places, Boston's Beacon Hill. Synergamous marriage, it seems, is pretty expensive. It is also not bigamy in a technical sense since a second marriage license is not fraudulently obtained. A second marriage license isn't obtained, period.

Rimmer's novel is a delightful and entertaining story with the literary limitations of his style and purposes. No researcher has yet produced a study of people who have admitted living synergamous marriages—the whole thing is just a fascinating idea. But Rimmer's ideas have a way of finding people to live them, and it probably will not be long before scholarly articles and books will be written about such people.

12. *Open-Ended Marriage.* The joys and values of monogamy are many and have long been praised by poets, preachers, and patriots. For some people, however, traditional monogamy has one especially serious limitation—mainly, sexual exclusiveness. Those who cherish traditional monogamy find security and the sign of mutual devotion in sexual fidelity. But there are those—and they are everywhere in this society—who do not equate sexual exclusiveness with marital fidelity. Repudiating the double standard, they enjoy intimacy, sensuality, and sometimes sex with other friends. Without shame and with trust in each other, the partners of an open-ended marriage enrich one another through their joy in loving and

growing. The energy of their love does not diminish for loving others—it is a synergistic process of emotional renewal and expansion.

Perhaps, of all of the lifestyles, OEM is most flexible and freeing. With a stable core of a special, primary, continuing interpersonal relationship, OEM can intermingle with other relational patterns while yet celebrating the enduring and creative aspects of monogamy. Those who practice OEM tend to believe that it offers new hope for the future of marriage.

*Modes of Sexual Behavior.* The preceding brief overview of alternative lifestyles is indicative of the variety of contemporary relational patterns. Perhaps all of them will endure and additional ones will be created. The twelve types again— in no especially significant order—are: traditional monogamy; child-free marriage; single parenthood; singlehood; communes; cohabitation; second-chance monogamy; swinging; family networks; group marriage; synergamous marriage; and open-ended marriage. Certainly there are difficulties, liabilities, and risks involved in all of them, and books will continue to be written advocating or denouncing each one. As confusing as the picture may seem, it becomes even more chaotic when we take into account the different modes of sexual behavior which may be combined with the various lifestyles. Other than traditional marriage, which is presumed to be heterosexual, all of the relational patterns can be lived by persons who practice exclusive heterosexuality, some degree of bisexuality, exclusive homosexuality, or even abstinence from genital sex. For example, it is theoretically possible to have a synergamous bisexual marriage with a person having a legal heterosexual marriage and a moral marriage to someone else of the same sex. Homosexual or lesbian marriages are not yet legally allowed, but that situation may change soon.

The thought of alternatives in modes of sexual behavior is probably shocking and disgusting to most people. Most of us have our own sexual prejudices and face each other with mental buttons programmed to read either "Gay Is Good," "Straight Is Super," or "Bisex Is Better." It can also be argued that exclusive heterosexuality and exclusive homosexuality are not alternatives, since no choice is involved: that both are a matter of genetic and/or hormonal factors and reinforcing experiences. Homosexuals and heterosexuals wage emotional and political war with each other over the "naturalness" of their conditions. Meanwhile bisexuals, whether predominantly heterosexual or predominantly homosexual, look upon exclusive sexual preference as rigid if not neurotic. And the advocates for abstinence are considered weird by everyone else. If only the stakes were not so high, the entire scene would be comical. It is instead tragic, tragic because there can be no winner unless all of us win the freedom to be our human selves regardless of our mode of sexual behavior. Without even having to understand the causality for the range of sexual expression between humans, it should be enough to recognize and accept the fact that there *is* a range, *all* of which is human.

## THE SEXUALITY PREFERENCE PROFILE

As people increasingly accept varieties of lifestyles and differences in modes of sexual behavior among consenting persons, the dichotomy between heterosexual and homosexual will become decreasingly significant. Even the Kinsey studies, which are about a quarter of a century old, indicate a range of bisexual behavior among men and women. It is time to broaden the perspective on sexual behavior to include other important categories; the sociable and the sensual as well as the strictly sexual. In order to increase awareness of a more comprehensive picture of sexual pluralism, the following exercise, the Sexuality Preference Profile (SPP), uses three categories—Sociable (I), Sensual (II), and Sexual (III)—in combination with four modalities—Hetero/Other Sex (A), Bi/Both Sexes (B), Homo/Same Sex (C), and Auto/Self Sex (D). It is important to realize that there are actually *eight* possible modalities for each category since a range of bisexuality can be indicated by one or two minuses, equality, or one or two pluses. For example: IIIB would mean equally bisexual; IIIB — would mean bisexual with occasional heterosexual behavior; IIIB — — would mean bisexual with frequent heterosexual experience; IIIB + would mean bisexual with occasional homosexual experience; and IIIB + + would indicate bisexuality with frequent homosexual genital contacts. All of the above sounds more complicated than it is when the SPP is charted. For purposes of the SPP exercise, the following category definitions are operable:

*Sociable* refers to enjoying the *company* of;
*Sensual* refers to enjoying the *touch* of;
*Sexual* refers to enjoying the *genitals* of.

These simplified definitions are somewhat arbitrary, but functional. It is not difficult to imagine, for example, that one can prefer socializing with one's own sex and be homosociable (I, C) yet be bisensual with a preference for frequent heterosensual touching (IIB — — ) while at the same time being exclusively heterosexual in genital activity and intercourse (IIIA). Obviously, there is an overlap of meaning in the categories; in fact, each level may incorporate the preceding ones within the same modality. A heterosexual, for instance, not only confines genital activity to members of the other sex, but usually would also enjoy the *touch* and the *company* of the partner.

A few comments must also be made about modality D, Auto/Self Sex since this option or condition is so often overlooked in discussions of ranges of sexual behavior. Auto/Self Sex does not imply negative evaluation. It is merely descriptive, referring to persons who regularly are or prefer to be by themselves (autosociable); who are not responsively touching persons (autosensual); and who do not participate in genital activity with another because of circumstances or choice (autosexual).

Since an explanation of the SPP can become complicated and tedious, simply turn to the exercise and try it out on a separate sheet of paper. Xerox copies can be made and the exercise shared either with a partner and/or within a group.

### SEXUALITY PREFERENCE PROFILE

|  | A (Other Sex) | % B (Both Sexes) % | | C (Same Sex) | D (Self Sex) |
|---|---|---|---|---|---|
| I | heterosociable | − − bisociable | + + | homosociable | autosociable |
| II | heterosensual | − − bisensual | + + | homosensual | autosensual |
| III | heterosexual | − − bisexual | + + | homosexual | autosexual |

#### MYSELF NOW

|  | A | B | C | D |
|---|---|---|---|---|
| I | — | — | — | — |
| II | — | — | — | — |
| III | — | — | — | — |

#### MYSELF AS I WOULD LIKE TO BE

|  | A | B | C | D |
|---|---|---|---|---|
| I | — | — | — | — |
| II | — | — | — | — |
| III | — | — | — | — |

#### HOW I SEE MY PARTNER NOW

|  | A | B | C | D |
|---|---|---|---|---|
| I | — | — | — | — |
| II | — | — | — | — |
| III | — | — | — | — |

### DISCUSSION QUESTIONS:

What Profile would you check for the "typical Male"?
What Profile would you check for the "typical Female"?
What Profile do you most disapprove of in both sexes (or least approve)?

## ALTERNATIVE LIFESTYLE CHECKLIST

___traditional monogamy

___child-free marriage

___single parenthood

___singlehood

___communes

___cohabitation

___second-chance monogamy

___swinging

___family networks

___group marriage

___synergamous marriage

___open-ended marriage

### INDICATE SELECTIONS ACCORDING TO THE FOLLOWING KEY:

A where you are now

B where you would like to be someday or "if you had it to do all over again"

C the lifestyle you think your partner would *really* prefer

D the lifestyle you most disapprove of (or least approve of)

If this Checklist is used with a partner, make copies and check separately, then share your reasons for—and feelings about—your selections to each other.

Note: both the SPP and the ALC can be used in small groups for discussion purposes. Have each person fill in forms anonymously but also indicating sex on upper right corner. Collect, shuffle, redistribute, and discuss in small groups. The groups can be divided according to sex, with the males dealing with the female responses and the females discussing the male responses. The two groups would offer commentary about the responses as a whole and then take turns asking each other questions. Other techniques for the use of the SPP and the ALC can, of course, be devised.

# CHAPTER SIX / DIVORCE AND THE
# OPEN-ENDED MARRIAGE

O O O O O O O O O O O O O O O O O O O O O O O O
O O O O O O O O O O O O O O O O O O O O O O O O
O O O O O O O O O O O O O O O O O O O O O O O O
O O O O O O O O O O O O O O O O O O O O O O O O
O O O O O O O O O O O O O O O O O O O O O O O O
O O O O O O O O O O O O O O O O O O O O O O O O
O O O O O O O O O O O O O O O O O O O O O O O O
O O O O O O O O O O O O O O O O O O O O O O O O
O O O O O O O O O O O O O O O O O O O O O O O O

Any book on marriage and intimacy must eventually deal
with the subject of divorce, for there are almost half as many
people terminating marriages each year as there are people
contracting marriages. The divorce rate in the United States
appears to be approaching 50 percent, which means that for
a given year there are 500 divorces for every 1,000 marriages.
The national average for the first quarter of 1972 was 455, as
compared to the 1971 divorce-marriage ratio of 428. And the
indications are that the divorce rate will continue to increase
as more states adopt humane or "liberal" divorce laws. There
seems to be more misery than intimacy in marriage.

Ironically, the climbing divorce rate represents not the
death of marriage, but its survival. Divorce is not the failure
of marriage but the agency for large-scale marriage turnover.
Divorced people escape, get thrown out of, or grow out of one
marriage, and most of them begin again the search for a new
marriage partner. Elizabeth Janeway describes the marriage-
divorce relationship in historical perspective.

" " " " "

Promiscuous or not, marriages go on getting made.
The reason is that our society long ago worked out a

pattern for adjusting marriage to the existence of a fair amount of extramarital sex as a social constant. As yet, this pattern has been flexible enough to absorb whatever changes have actually occurred.

The pattern—it's no great discovery—is one that preserves the social stability of marriage as an institution by letting married people change partners. Though prostitution was certainly the greatest support of nineteenth-century marriage, a percentage of our ancestors, like the Marri, maintained their households by staying with husbands or wives by setting up relatively permanent adulterous relationships on the outside, so that marriage and adultery went on together in a symbiotic relationship. Even during the nineteenth century, however, the American pattern began to diverge from this earlier European arrangement and to become what it is today. Here it's usual for marriages that turn bad to be followed not simply by extramarital affairs, but by divorce and remarriage between lovers. For us, it is not adultery that supports marriage, or prostitution, but divorce; and this situation began to develop a good long time ago.[1]

" " " " "

If it is true, as Janeway suggests, that we have moved through a process of surreptitiously sanctioned supports for the continued survival of marriage—prostitution, adultery, and divorce—then it is intriguing to see the open-ended marriage as the next step in the process. Divorced persons, however, have for too long suffered the condemnation of prostitutes and adulterers, and it is time for that judgmental attitude to be eradicated from civic law, if not in the minds of all people. Instead, divorce can be seen as an extreme form of an interpersonal process which is common to strong individuals and relationships. This process can be called *distancing* and satisfies a need for private emotional space. Before exploring this process, however, it may be of value to examine some dynamics between divorce and religion.

## RELIGION AND DIVORCE

While financial support for organized religion is decreasing and the numbers of members are declining, the search for religious meaning and spiritual experience is intensifying in our culture—perhaps even around the globe. People everywhere are seeking wholeness of being, the courage to risk value-venturing, the joy of celebrating life and affirming each other. It is incredible—wonderfully amazing—that so many scientists and psychologists, for example, sound like preachers announcing the good news of a new age for humankind (when they are not sounding like doomsday prophets), urging every person to actualize his/her full potential, to love, to pleasure, to laugh, and to join together to save an abused friendly planet. It's a fantastic time to be on earth.

Organized or institutionalized religion, however, cannot be ignored entirely for the forceful reason that it still influences our attitudes toward sex, marriage, and the family. This influence may be diminishing, but nevertheless it is still pervasive. It has also been destructive. It has spread fear, shame, irrational guilt, and promoted self-disgust with regard to sensual and sexual enjoyment. It has made divorced people agonize with a crippling sense of failure and betrayal. Homosexuals and lesbians are shamefully deprived of their participation in the religious community just as they are robbed of their civil right to legal marital union. The heterosexual presumptions of Jewish and Christian theologies deny lesbians and homosexuals the religious celebration of their love, a blasphemous prejudice which can no longer be sanctified. The male sexist basis of those same theologies has stifled the human potential of both sexes. Much more could be said about the inadequacy of religious groups to cope constructively— never mind taking a leading part—with changing relational patterns and modes of sexual behavior. It is not enough, however, merely to indict organized religion for its failures. What is more creative is to challenge it to serve, to work with, to inspire, to reform itself for the sake of all people in their search for more joyful lives and a better world. Let us take as an example of such a challenge the critical issue of divorce and a new way in which religious communities could respond to that issue.

## THE RITE OF DIVORCE

Divorce is a reality of contemporary life, and it is time for religious groups to take positive steps toward applying their healing ministry to those who choose or are driven into marital divorce.

Most churches are still in the inept, fumbling stage of helping contemporary men, women, and children cope effectively with the ethical dimensions and personal problems of sex behavior, marriage, and family life. Clergypersons and churches do not yet even seek to establish positive programs in love education for youth (as distinct from just sex-education), premarital counseling, and postmarital seminars. Ultimately, of course, such systematic approaches to these essential dimensions of interpersonal relationships will prove to be the best form of divorce prevention. Meanwhile, however, as churches go on grappling with these programs and as clergypersons increasingly seek the proper training for competence in these areas of interpersonal relationships, marriages continue to split, and more and more people stagger confused, hurt, and guilt-laden from the wreckage of broken homes. Though divorce should not be casually accepted, churches can do much more than look sadly upon the phenomenon. By incorporating divorce into the rites of the church they can bring direction and healing into troubled lives.

## THEOLOGICAL CONSIDERATIONS OF TRADITIONAL MARRIAGE

Divorce in the church requires, of course, a theological acceptance of marital separation with possible remarriage. An understanding of divorce involves an understanding of marriage. Church divorce would, for instance, necessitate at least one change in the marriage rite. Before the pronouncement of those traditional last words, one sentence should be added. Preceding the admonishment "And those whom God hath joined together, let no man put asunder" should be the counsel, "Those whom God and circumstance hath made incompatible, let no person judge inseparable." Only divine wisdom can ascertain the true oneness of a marital union.

Marriage is, however, a sacramental union. In striving for the harmony and unity of "one-flesh," a male and a female are blessed with the opportunity of co-creating with God a higher order of humanhood. This, essentially, is one of the meanings of the Creation Myth, which tells us that Man and Woman are created for each other and that in their complementarity they together are Human Being. Creative marriage is a cosmic event! There is something deeply saddening in every marital break-up precisely because of the missed opportunity for two persons to temper the quality of their being in the existential heat of the marital forge. Those who persevere, who struggle to commune beyond the inevitable isolation of unique self-hood, who accept their trials as challenges, who share and nurture common values in the wondrous venture of life, they are those who create a higher order of being.

But particular lives do not follow theological criteria, psychological norms, or poetic visions. We live as well in sweat, in tears, in vulnerable flesh, possessed of innumerable anxieties and irrationalities. And while there is sustenance in the truth that God created male and female for the communion of "one flesh," there is also saving grace in the truth that He/ She did not create specific men and women for particular marriages. Almost everyone had some measure of free choice in each other; some happen to have chosen badly. Some even chose well, but outgrew the relationship. While some people are forever alarmed at the high divorce rates, it is perhaps more profound to wonder at the ability of so many men and women to live reasonably happy and worthwhile lives in spite of the circumstances of their marriages. So it is that some marriages do not last—indeed, some linger too long—regardless of the best intentions and the most truthful promises. And in such cases there are ethical, social, and psychological factors which the religious community must consider in divorce if it is to provide a healing, caring ministry.

## THE SACRAMENTAL NATURE OF CHURCH DIVORCE

The religious community celebrates and commemorates, through symbol and ceremony, the most significant events in the maturation cycle: birth, marriage, and finally death. There are even rites for such important occasions as serious illness, school graduation, or moving into a new home. Why not, then, recognize liturgically the crucial impact of the divorce experience? Even today, for all of the supposed sophistication toward the subject of divorce, two persons in the process of divorce will need the support of their friends and religious community almost more than they will at any other time in their lives. One day in the past, the two stood before the same or a similar convenanted community and vowed lifelong commitment to each other. The discovery that those vows cannot be maintained between them is, at best, a terribly painful realization. All too often, the two persons must suffer in silence and isolation, too ashamed to hope for understanding and help from friends or church. But the religious community ought always to uphold its people for better or for worse, and it should stand behind a couple in their hour of parting. The man, woman, and children, if any, ought to be accepted and upheld without judgment, and, in their new status, reintegrated into the community.

The religious ceremony of divorce is worthwhile not only for support, but also for the testimony of forgiveness. Persons who are divorcing need the opportunity to forgive each other explicitly, and they can testify to that forgiveness in the presence of the congregation. They also need some assurance of compassion in the sight of God and forgiveness from the community. And, furthermore, they need also to forgive the community for its possible failure to be of help when help was needed. This dimension of mutual forgiveness is the most important differentiation between a church divorce and a civil divorce. It is also the most crucial factor in preventing the divorce experience from embittering the two for life and from warping the understanding of the children.

Finally, in addition to support and forgiveness the church ceremony should also bestow a blessing upon the man and woman, who must now strive for new relationships. A benediction upon them is the church's way of testifying to their right to hope for new dimensions and experiences of love and happiness.

## CHURCH DIVORCE AS
## DIVORCE PREVENTION

It is unfortunate but understandable that parishioners do not consult the clergyperson when they are considering divorce. Such couples, as troubled as they are, would rather suffer in silence than share the problem with their clergyperson, for they assume that the clergyperson will have only one goal in mind: to preach them together again. But, just as in premarital counseling the clergyperson ought not to judge whether or not the two should marry, so too, in divorce counseling, the clergyperson ought not to judge whether or not the couple should divorce.

Ethical, religious preparation for divorce could, however, quite often serve to involve the couple in such a degree of mutual consideration and essential communication that divorce would no longer seem a sensible solution to their marital problems. As two persons explore with their clergyperson the sacramental dimensions of marriage, as they realize that their union has created an "ineradicable" relationship, as they consider responsibly the needs of their children, and as they achieve some insight into the nature of their problems, divorce will often be recognized as an immature escape. On the other hand, in those cases where divorce is a reasonable and beneficial resolution of severe difficulties, the couple must still be helped to understand all of the above factors so that their parting is mutually compassionate and so that they part in a state of self-realization rather than in a state of self-destruction.

It is time for our churches to help clear away the shame by which couples are overwhelmed when they have marital problems. Some people try so hard to cover up in order to avoid gossip or social disgrace that they set the conditions leading to divorce. What is it about church people and religious leaders which fails to inspire the sharing of such basic human trials?

## THE CHURCH'S AUTHORITY TO DIVORCE

It is not only the obligation of the church to have a rite of divorce, but it should also be the right of the church to grant divorce. Present forms of civil divorce in courts of law are degrading, shameful, defeating procedures which ought to be abolished. Divorce is a human event which should not take place in a courtroom or a city hall. Lawyers and judges should be released from this misplaced responsibility. We must also inquire as to what ethical or moral right the state has to determine the conditions or grounds for divorce. The various laws which define grounds for divorce are vestiges of an older morality which is no longer generally accepted. Many of the divorce laws of the United States are hypocritical and a travesty of justice. The deceit and sensationalism which they force upon those desirous of divorce destroy all integrity and honesty, making of divorce courts stinking pits of deception and bitterness. Civil divorce laws and procedures contribute nothing to healing and growth, personally or socially. At best, divorce courts are improperly used to uphold the antidivorce prejudices and opinions of various denominations and sects.

There are, of course, legitimate social and civic interests which the courts seek to defend, promote, and safeguard. The rights of the sued party and the legal guarantees for responsible child care are certainly their proper concerns. These matters obviously do belong to the legal profession. Since both marriage and divorce are not solely personal acts, but involve social consequences and ramifications, it should be expected that reasonable social demands will be involved. Note, however, that in civil marriage the state can make no attempt to ascertain suitability of marriage. So too, in divorce, it should be possible for two persons simply to register their intentions and to be granted a divorce decree upon the fulfilling of minimum, essential, social, and legal obligations. The reasons for divorce are personal and private and should be respected as such. Most lawyers and magistrates are deeply concerned to help their clients over and above technical legal services, and they should continue to explore ways and means of encouraging persons in divorce proceedings to seek marriage counseling. Some lawyers are even trained to offer such professional counseling service. But these human considerations must remain persuasive-voluntary rather than legal-coercive. The only restrictions or conditions which society should be allowed to impose on both marriage and divorce should be medical or legal, but never moral or religious.

In marriage, couples have an option between civil or church ceremonies. The same option should be available in divorce. It is the ethical and value dimensions of human relationships which are the explicit concerns of religious communions, and it is precisely these dimensions which make church weddings and divorces of greater meaning and worth to the individuals concerned. Obviously, however, not all religions and churches share the same theological framework, and it should be left to such groups to develop the specific conditions and procedures for their rites of divorce. A couple divorced according to the practice of their religion would then file their divorce with the state. State registration would involve legal counsel and service in the matter of satisfying requirements for the care of children and other legal and social conditions. Actually, this registration and legal procedure would probably best precede the grant and rite of divorce by the church. The courts and the legal profession would then be free to devote their time and abilities to the many other pressing judicial matters with which they are overwhelmed. Religion, society, and—most important of all—the human beings involved, would all greatly benefit from the development and availability of church-granted divorces.

Is it possible for such a system to be worked out? Undoubtedly it would be extremely difficult for many reasons. Just the establishment of sane and uniform divorce laws would require immense effort. Nevertheless, the cooperation between jurisprudence and religion in the evolution of such a new approach to divorce can make a great contribution to the renewal of family life in our society.

## SELF-HELP AND THE PROCESS OF EMOTIONAL SPACING

Whether or not organized religion—which pretends to care so much about family life—will ever respond creatively to the reality of divorce, it is still possible and necessary for all persons contemplating divorce to help themselves. Many terrible marriages are terminated to the relief of both parties. Many conventionally good marriages are also broken because of growing, discontenting awareness on the part of one or both partners.[2] There are countless reasons for divorce with various degrees of suffering and happiness involved. It is likely, however, that there would be fewer unnecessary divorces if people could learn the art of emotional spacing. In their eagerness for togetherness and mutual sharing, too many marital partners begin to live life through each other and lose their independence and individuality. They become possessive of one another (see the discussion of possessive jealousy) and/or the relationship stabilizes on a level of sophisticated stagnation: conventionally successful, but boring and suffocating. Or there are endless irritations which lead to irrational quarrels from which neither partner benefits. Without emotional spacing "bad" marriages become unendurable and "good" marriages become merely bearable.

There are two aspects or qualities of emotional spacing, both of which often cause problems in interpersonal relationships. One of them is *detachment* and the other is *distance.* They imply each other and seem to be contradictory to involvement and commitment, but, paradoxically, emotional spacing and relational union can creatively coexist.

Detachment is the awareness that one cannot live anyone else's life for them; that growth and learning cannot be fully communicated and passed on, for it must inevitably be experienced personally. Even as a loved one agonizes or suffers, our involvement can only be supportive but we can never take that person's place. *Or even want to do so,* for the integrity and wisdom of the other require personal growth through crisis. No one should be deprived the dignity of spiritual or psychological agony, for it is through such genuine suffering that the self finds identity and direction.

Developing the capacity to be detached from others rather than being overly protective or possessive also requires the ability for self-detachment. This is one of the most mysterious characteristics of the human being, that the self can stand outside of the self and critically observe and correct or challenge the self. Self-detachment with honesty, humility, and humor makes life a risky but exciting venture. Once the self becomes an open, value-venturing being, both suffering and ecstasy become more intense, and the days of living are fulfilled rather than being wasted or thrown away. The person who has this ability for detachment isn't necessarily highly regarded by others. In his classic study of healthy, self-actualizing people, Abraham Maslow observed:

" " " " "

In social relations with most people, detachment creates certain troubles and problems. It is easily interpreted by "normal" people as coldness, snobbishness, lack of affection, unfriendliness, or even hostility. By contrast, the ordinary friendship relationship is more clinging, more demanding, more desirous of reassurance, compliment, support, warmth, and exclusiveness. It is true that self-actualizing people do not need others in the ordinary sense. But since this being needed or being missed is the usual earnest of friendship, it is evident that detachment will not easily be accepted by average people.[3]

" " " " "

If the detachment aspect of emotional spacing can be said to represent the importance of recognizing the self of others, then the distance aspect of emotional spacing can be said to represent the importance of recognizing one's own self. Self-detachment leads to the periodic need for distancing— moving away from intense intimacy from the other(s) to get in touch with one's self. Distancing is even more of a threat to others than is detaching, for it is most often interpreted as rejection and sometimes it is interpreted as emotional breakdown. Distancing is more than a need for privacy (privacy can be considered a briefer and milder form of distancing); it is the self turning in to seek renewal, refreshment, insight, inspiration, and energy for creativity. It is not a rejection of others, but a temporary return to the well-springs of the self.

## EMOTIONAL SPACING AND DIVORCE

Emotional spacing is vital to any kind of creative marriage and is especially imperative in an open-ended marriage. It has an important relationship to divorce precisely for the reason that some marriages which terminate in divorce had great potential for the well-being and growth of those concerned if only the partners had developed the ability for emotional spacing. It is sadly ironic that those who refuse to risk spacing end separating. There is, of course, no "how-to-do-it" prescription for every couple or group, and obviously, not everyone will have the same degree of need for emotional spacing. Nevertheless, the major point is that we do not *always* have to be the same person to each other, for there are times to be lovers, friends, challengers, and strangers to one another. Marriage partners and lovers may even choose to live apart from each other periodically or to take separate vacations occasionally, or to have their own nights out or weeks away. Arrangements for physical privacy and separateness can facilitate emotional spacing, but even if a couple or group remains together most of the time, the dynamics of emotional spacing in the relationship ought to be practiced. Interesting problems arise when, for example, one partner wants to be lover at the same time the other partner wants to be stranger, but such differences in intimacy level can be fun as well as frustrating. At least, the "you-don't-love-me-anymore" game doesn't have to be played. It is so much more creative and enjoyable for couples to communicate expectations, needs, desires, values, and goals to each other rather than reducing everything to a matter of "love." Are you "out of love" when you are angry or resentful toward your lover? Are you "out of love" when you feel distant from your partner but close to someone else? Couples who have so much going for them in their marital relationship will often convince themselves that "love is dead" when emotional spacing is experienced and misunderstood.

## DIVORCE AND OEM

Instead of looking at the divorce route as the only option to a stale or dull marriage, some couples with a relatively high degree of positive emotional investment in each other might seriously consider experimenting with the OEM model. The process of renegotiating the covenantal or contractual basis of the marriage can be an exhilarating venture, painful at times, but in a way healing. It is reasonable to assume that in some cases experimentation with OEM will lead to divorce. It is also reasonable to hypothesize that OEM as a conscious pre-divorce experiment will lead to the renewal of some marriages. In all cases, the reasons and motivations for experimentation will be essential to success or failure. In the situation where a couple is considering divorce, what can be lost by discovering new dimensions of each other? OEM requires cooperation and communication, both of which are essential to good divorces, where parents maintain common concern for their children and for each other. Why not, then, try cooperation and communication in a new context? Many marriage counselors would be of the opinion that direct and outright divorce is preferable to any compromise with extramarital affairs.[4] This is, however, a value preference which isn't valuable in all cases, especially in the situation of open-ended marriage. Warm sexual relationships—casual and/or long-term—with others can be part of a marriage-enrichment process, but even if the couple should continue to decide for divorce, they can help each other explore the new world of dating, flirting, courting, and sexual relations. They can be supportive of each other morally, financially, and in other matters of household and child care during a difficult transitional period—a period which can be a new beginning for each rather than a catastrophic marital and family crash. "Extramarital" sexual experiences serve many purposes both "good" and "bad" in marriages. And it is encouraging that scholars are looking at the positive functions of such experiences. Perhaps there will soon be developed the techniques and programs to utilize a transitional form of open-ended marriage which will lead to happier lives by renewing marriages or making divorce a constructive step in realizing self-potential.

*The J & P Exercise:* Before you read the following chapter, "Beyond Jealousy and Possessiveness," take a sheet of paper and write a paragraph about your last remembered experience of intense jealousy. Think about it for awhile, and try to recapture what you thought and felt the last time you had an experience which you could call "jealousy." Put aside your paragraph (or more) after you have finished it and read the chapter, returning to your paper as the last paragraph of the chapter.

# CHAPTER SEVEN / BEYOND JEALOUSY AND POSSESSIVENESS

O O O O O O O O O O O O O O O O O O O O O O O O O O O
O O O O O O O O O O O O O O O O O O O O O O O O O O
O O O O O O O O O O O O O O O O O O O O O O O O O O O
O O O O O O O O O O O O O O O O O O O O O O O O O O O
O O O O O O O O O O O O O O O O O O O O O O O O O O O
O O O O O O O O O O O O O O O O O O O O O O O O O O O
O O O O O O O O O O O O O O O O O O O O O O O O O O O
O O O O O O O O O O O O O O O O O O O O O O O O O O O
O O O O O O O O O O O O O O O O O O O O O O O O O O O

"I the Lord your God, am a jealous God" (Deut. 5.09, RSV)
"Love is not jealous or boastful" (I Cor. 13.04, RSV)

To those who are not familiar with the complexities of Jewish and Christian theology, it certainly looks as if St. Paul one-upped God in wisdom. The transposition of the above biblical sentences implies that the boastfully jealous God is without love, and provides an interesting example of the varied and confusing meanings of "jealousy."

It is astonishing that so little has been written in recent years about such a universal and powerful emotion; an emotion which has triggered horrendous violence in human experience. Religious mythology, the theater, and the classics are suffused with themes of jealousy and its consequences. In the ancient Greek pantheon, Hera is the prototype of the jealous bitch who constantly nags husband Zeus about his incurable and outrageous philandering. The second-century Latin writer Apuleius contrives the gripping story of a vengeful mother who is bitterly jealous of Psyche, her son Cupid's lover. And among Shakespeare's gory tragedies, Othello, whose insane jealousy drives him to murder his faithful wife, Desdemona, is an unforgettable characterization. And yet, in works of psychology, sociology, anthropology, and philosophy, scant attention is given to the analysis and significance of jealousy. Perhaps jealousy has simply gone underground to allow a superficial social accommodation of changing marital partners.

Jealousy is a critical clue to models of marriage. It is an emotional response which is situational and learned. Its primary function has been to reinforce the sexually exclusive factor in traditional monogamy. But as models of monogamy change, the expression of jealousy loses its value and may even be considered inappropriate behavior and a sign of emotional immaturity. In 1958, for example, David Mace could write: "Jealousy can be a very destructive force in a marriage. Yet we won't understand it aright unless we recognize at the start that it is essentially quite natural and, in its right place, good and useful. We are all endowed with certain protective emotions. . . . Jealousy [is one of them]—it makes you watchful over the relationships upon which your security and happiness depend."[1] In 1972, the husband and wife authors of *Open Marriage: A New Life Style for Couples* state forthrightly: "No matter how little or how much, jealousy is never a good or constructive feeling. It may show you care, but what you are caring for is too much for yourself, and not enough for your mate."[2] Which viewpoint is correct? Possibly both. Something has happened to marriage in the fourteen-year interval between those two statements. With greater equalitarianism, and new covenantal or contractual options within marriage, the function of jealousy is changing if not disappearing. Sociologist Jessie Bernard clearly understands the process when she asserts: "If monogamous marriage as we have known it in the past is in process of change, there may be less and less need for jealousy to buttress it, and less and less socialization of human beings to experience it or move to control it."[3] In traditional monogamy, jealousy may be attributed a positive value; the lack of it, for example, being interpreted as indifference, uncaring, or unloving. In open-ended marriage, however, jealousy has no positive function and is not valued; it is at best, a symptom of tension and poor communication in the relationship.

For those who are strongly motivated to outgrow jealousy, three questions are critical: what is the nature of jealousy; can jealousy be totally and permanently eradicated from a person; and how do persons go about understanding and deconditioning jealous feeling and behavior patterns? Before answering such questions, it is helpful to assume a casual and positive attitude toward jealousy in persons: it's there; it's something to deal with; somebody is experiencing deep feelings, and the task is to understand them in the context of what that person is trying to learn or communicate. Joan Constantine and Larry Constantine, in their research and work with multilateral or group marriages make observations about jealousy applicable to other alternative lifestyles. "If all jealousy is simply rejected as undesirable or immature, the affect goes underground and interferes with group functioning and the exchange of other feelings. If jealousy is lauded or facilely accepted, growth in important dimensions can be hindered. Thus it is necessary for participants in group marriages to differentiate among various forms of jealousy. Jealousy, if approached properly, becomes an opportunity to discover new information about individuals and their relationships."[4] Jealousy must be recognized, admitted, and worked with if it is to lead to personal growth and relational enrichment.

What, then, is the meaning of jealousy and how can it be recognized? While nineteenth-century American dictionaries clearly indicated both negative and positive meanings of the word, it is interesting that the 1970 paperback edition of *The American Heritage Dictionary of the English Language* gives predominantly negative denotations of "jealous." To be jealous is to be "1. Fearful of loss of position or affection. 2. Resentful in rivalry; envious. 3. Possessively watchful; vigilant." What seems clear is that the word itself has borne the burden of too many meanings; there is a great deal of legitimate difference and semantic confusion surrounding its historical usage. The trend also seems to be to use it only in a negative way. Regardless of how contemporary lexicographers define it, jealousy is more than a word; it is usually a gut-feeling experience filled with anxiety, resentment, threat, fear, and other hurtful emotions. It comes like a flash flood, undoubtedly causing various physiological manifestations. Jealousy is a complex emotion, and perhaps the only way to understand it and to control it—not eliminate it—is to analyze its various forms. Perhaps, if we analyze its various forms, we will find that jealousy can be defused of its demonic potential.

The following is a typology of jealousy which does not include the archaic positive usages, or the classifications of "healthy" or "romantic" jealousy. It is intended for use by all those who are disturbed by unwanted feelings of jealousy —who want to work toward eliminating it in relationships. In the open-ended marriage, jealousy has no creative purpose. This is to recognize, however, that in a lengthy transitional period, persons conscientiously experimenting with OEM and other lifestyles will already be conditioned to be jealous under various circumstances and will have to relearn new emotional and behavioral patterns. The task, then, is to recognize, understand, and deal openly and creatively with whatever kind of jealousy is experienced. It must also be emphasized that the forms of jealousy are interrelated with some common causes and consequences.

## ENVY-JEALOUSY VERSUS REALITY LIVING

While some scholars make a case for differentiating jealousy from envy, it is more fruitful to consider enviousness as a variety of jealousy. The terms are often used synonymously and defined as such in contemporary dictionaries. Although an 1886 American dictionary states that "Envy is a base passion, and never used, like jealousy, in a good sense," it is quite probable that of all the forms of jealousy, most persons can easily empathize with envy. Early American lexicographers were clergymen or theologically astute scholars who understood and accepted biblical morality. They knew that the "jealous God" of Scripture was zealous for the righteousness of His people, that the quality of that jealousy was commitment and caring. They also knew the biblical commandment against covetousness—desiring wives or cattle not lawfully theirs. To be envious, therefore, was to break the Commandments.

To feel envy, however, is not actually to steal anyone's wife, livestock, or other possessions—it is wishful thinking. Everyone experiences it countless times. Someone else is always better-looking, more personable, more talented, richer, luckier, more intelligent, more courageous, happier, more lovable, or loved, or more valuable for the human race. What one envies reveals not simply what one would like to have, but often what one would like to be. But if envious wishful thinking is not soon transcended by realistic, dedicated work toward desired goals, or by honest, possibly humorous rejection of the specific source of envy, it can lead to crippling resentment and self-pity. A Boston newspaper interview with a young couple living an open-ended relationship probed the difficulties of such a lifestyle. The young husband was enthusiastic and self-assured but did admit to one difficulty. He admitted to being jealous on occasions when a male friend of his wife's would take her to restaurants he could not afford. Although the husband used the word "jealous," what he was more specifically feeling was envy-jealousy. He wanted to have the money to provide experiences as enjoyable for his wife as any other male could provide. The nature of envy, as well as other forms of jealousy, is that it always needs *more* to satisfy it. The young man seemed to be able to express his wishes honestly, without rancor or self-defeating pride. But if he had lacked the ability to be in touch with his feelings, to deal with them openly, he would have set conditions for the failure of his marital relationship.

Perhaps certain types of personalities are prone to certain types of jealousy, but everyone at times has reflected on his/her given life-situation and looked with envy on greener fields. If one faces the reality of one's own limitations and circumstances, however, anger and/or aspiration will be appropriately directed rather than deflected inwardly causing depression and/or debilitating self-pity.

## POSSESSIVE-JEALOUSY VERSUS AUTONOMY

Emotional space for each partner to be autonomous is a necessary condition for any type of creative marriage or intimate relationship. For the recognition and growth of our own self—our integrity or wholeness—we need emotional space. Poet Kahlil Gibran advises lovers: "Love one another, but make not a bond of love. Rather let it be a moving sea between the shores of your souls," and he speaks of "spaces in togetherness." This is startling for young lovers to hear, for they think of their love as an eternal bond. But Gibran jars the thoughtful into serious consideration of unspoken realities. Very few couples, however, consider the meanings of a traditional pronouncement of marriage: "I now pronounce you man and wife." Man and *wife?* Apparently men, clergy and grooms, are loath to create such a binding role as husband, for why not say "husband and wife"? Clergymen would sound ridiculous saying, "I now pronounce you Man and Woman," though such a declaration has intriguing possibilities. In any case, such a pronouncement would grant the Man nothing—which is not what traditional marriage was created for. It is the woman who is *given* in marriage by her father or other male kinsman. The traditional wedding service, deceptively elegant and sentimental, is the ritual wherein the father of the bride pays his property tax and transfers the title of ownership.

It is no wonder that people cry at weddings—there are a number of profound reasons why tears are appropriate.

Possessiveness is culturally sanctioned but is nevertheless a dehumanizing process. The possessive person does not know the inherent value or even the identity of the person possessed. The possessor is also possessed by private versions of reality—a reality requiring order, reassurance, and respect from without, and a sense of power and control. This allows for predictability, homage, and manipulation, but negates the qualities of spontaneity, authentic self-esteem, and mutuality of relationship. By perceiving the other merely as an extension of one's own life—even when romantically intended—that other person is deprived of dignity, individuality, and freedom to be and become with integrity. Possessiveness can, of course, be symbiotic in the sense that both spouses build their lives around it and feed off each other. This is so much the case that possessive marriage has superseded religion as the "opiate of the masses"; it is a stupefied security without joy, enthusiasm, or adventure.

The double-standard reinforces the sanctions for possessiveness in accordance with the best interests of males. When the male is possessive-jealous, the female is supposed to feel proud and grateful. When the female is possessive-jealous the male flaunts it as a sign of his desirability and attractiveness as long as the female doesn't push too hard. But when the female becomes too demanding she is demeaned as being nothing but a castrating bitch.

Possessive-jealousy is perhaps the most raging and wrathful form of jealousy, leading to acts of cruel vengeance and even murder. "You belong to me and if you cross me I'll get even with you. If I can't have you nobody is going to have you." That sentiment sounds as if it comes from one of those unbelievably trite movies. Yet, the sentiments of possessive people *are* unfortunately trite, and potentially destructive.

Is it possible to be monogamously committed to someone without possessiveness? We pose the question because many couples seem to confuse commitment with belonging to. Possessiveness is commitment without trust. Conversely, commitment with trust celebrates the autonomy of the other; rejoices in the uniqueness of the other; is aware of the privacy needs of the other. There need be no contradiction between mutual commitment and the mutual allowance for emotional space.

## EXCLUSION-JEALOUSY VERSUS SHARING

The most painful type of jealousy is exclusion-jealousy: being left out of a lovely or critical experience of a loved one. While it's true that *every* experience is unique to the person undergoing or feeling it—since no two persons will ever see, feel, understand and value a shared experience in precisely the same way—it is nevertheless true that there is something beautiful and important about a couple going through something together. For those who seek to live a joyous open-ended marriage, exclusion-jealousy will be the most difficult interpersonal barrier they must overcome. It is a formidable hurdle which occasions the most sublime exhilaration once cleared. Over the long course, it reoccurs at intervals but it becomes easier to take and soon becomes a pleasurable challenge.

It's easy to feel jealous when you are excluded. It's not a matter of wanting to deny one's partner a new or enjoyable experience with someone else. Rather one wants to be included in the experience. It is also not a matter of possessiveness as such. For one can be genuinely nonpossessive and yet be overcome by exclusion-jealousy. It can happen for two reasons: being shut out of a good time and/or not having similar pleasure with another while the spouse is involved elsewhere. It sometimes comes down to a matter of, "Damn it, how come you have all the opportunities while I seem to be stuck in a rut?" Or it could be something like, "Why did you go there with your friend when you never like to go there with me?" Exclusion-jealousy is especially intense when a partner feels—or is—neglected in comparison to the time, finances, interest, and enthusiasm the spouse is lavishing upon someone else. Then there are those inevitable disappointing conflicts in plans when one partner says, "Oh, by the way, I'll be out with so-and-so on next Thursday evening" and the other replies, "Hell, I was hoping we could do something special together that evening." That "something special" is usually quite specific and it means changing plans with the friend or disappointing the spouse. With a little practice, however, couples can avoid such conflicts.

Couples living an open-ended marriage will handle the problems of exclusion-jealousy in various ways, including an attempt never to exclude each other. Some couples, for example, feel strongly that they can always include the spouse, even when the spouse is not present, by sharing their experiences verbally and by having their friends always meet the spouse. This inclusive approach might possibly work for couples with similar needs who are able to verbalize experiences and always enjoy meeting each other's friends. Other couples, however, will not find this a satisfying solution—their needs for privacy and emotional space may be strong, they may find verbal analysis of their experiences superficial. Such couples would rather confront the fact of exclusion directly. They are willing to say, "Yes, it's true we have experiences with others from which our spouse is excluded. We don't experience all of each other's intimate friendships, but we rejoice in the persons we are and in the richness of our relationships. We simply have to learn to live with the freedom to have partially separate lives—and we really wouldn't want it any other way." Ultimately, it is not so much a question of just sharing each other.

## COMPETITION-JEALOUSY
## VERSUS SPECIALNESS

Marriage partners who are self-actualizing may at times be jealous of each other's achievements and will compete for recognition and success. At its best, this can be creative tension; at its worst, undercutting oneupmanship.

The arena of competition, however, is not restricted to status and success. This is not to say that this contest is unimportant or trivial. On the contrary, it's imperative for women to refuse being consigned to supportive roles, to unleash their full creative potential for the benefit of themselves and for all people. If this kind of competition makes men uncomfortable, that's *their* problem. Women for too long have apologized for bruising frail male egos, and such men are just going to have to grow up and stop expecting their wives to be their mothers.

Negative forms of competition stem from a lack of self-confidence or self-esteem leading to jealousy of the partner's achievements, attractiveness, friends, or sexual performance. Behind competition-jealousy is the attitude: "You think I'm not good enough for you, but I'll show you!" This projection of inadequacy demands constant reassurance from the partner, but the reassurance is always suspected of being mere condescension. What is needed to overcome this form of jealousy is the development of self-esteem in combination with the sense of being essentially *special* to one's lover. This sense of specialness rests on the attitude: "Sure, I'm aware you know some fantastic people who also think you're great, but that makes me happy for you because I also know I'm uniquely special to you, that the quality of our relationship is one of the highest shared values in our lives." To be glad for the other without feeling like a second-rate person does indeed require a high degree of self-esteem. And, ironically, that self-esteem is easier to develop when two people lovingly help each other to be special through mutual respect, sensual pleasuring, admiration, approval, support, and sometimes forgiveness.

## EGOTISM-JEALOUSY VERSUS ROLE FREEDOM

Role flexibility or interchangeability is a new personal freedom and a new feature of contemporary interpersonal relationships.

The rigid stereotypes of masculinity and femininity have already been shattered, opening new avenues for self-realization and interpersonal openness. There are, to be sure, casualties of this shattering of sex stereotypes, and there are those who defensively hide from its impact. A time of transition is confusing and difficult for many. Nevertheless, the change is relentless and there is no turning back to the comforting absurdities of conformist man-woman, woman-woman, or man-man relationships. There is a new role freedom for all persons who will no longer allow themselves and their potentialities to be defined by cultural conformity or the insensitive expectations of others. This freedom also allows problems to surface: men who become enraged or embarrassed because their wives challenge them in public; women who become enraged or embarrassed because their husbands seem openly affectionate to other males. Examples of anger or embarrassment over a conflict in role expectations are endless.

Egotism-jealousy is a denial of role freedom. It is, in a sense, wanting a girl/boy just like the girl/boy that married dear old dad/mom. Rather than see the crisis of role interchangeability as an opportunity for growth, some people are ashamed of their "unfeminine" wives or "unmasculine" (note that the word is usually "effeminate") husbands and are jealous of other people who have "ideal" husbands/wives.

Egotism-jealousy can also be turned against the spouse with the ability for role flexibility who exposes the rigidity of the less flexible partner.

Egotism-jealousy is similar to envy-jealousy but is more specifically related to one's ability or inability to expand one's ego awareness and role flexibility. When both men and women can be persons in whatever ways that make them happiest regardless of what and how tradition defines them sexually, they will invest less of their egos in social roles and status. Can you imagine a time when baby boys and baby girls will be born free?

## FEAR-JEALOUSY VERSUS SECURITY

Jealousy can be just plain fear: fear of losing someone special; fear of being lonely, of being rejected. To the extent that one's own value depends upon a partner's devotion, one will be vulnerable to the fear of desertion. If there is a classic form of jealousy, this probably is it, although an equally strong case can be made for possessive-jealousy. Fear-jealousy doubts the commitment of the other; it breeds on insecurity. It torments with anxiety and anguish. "What if my lover finds someone else better than me? What will happen to me?" Underlying such fearful feelings is the assumption that one is satisfying to the lover only as a desirable product—when something "better" comes along one will be abandoned. It's a hell of a way to live, but fear-jealousy is one foundation on which many marriages precariously endure.

The only security in a healthy relationship is to be a person, not a product. None of us is desirable or enjoyable in every way on every day, and if our relationships depend on the fear of having our lovers discover the attractiveness of others, then we do indeed shape dull and emotionally crippled lovers. Let your lover look at you with all of your blemishes and shortcomings and let your relationship be a dynamic exploration in life and becoming rather than a wedding exchange of personality packages. The strongest and most joyful relationships are those in which partners are not afraid to let each other go; attempting to control the duration of a relationship because of insecurity sacrifices the magnificence of every *now*. Bless and celebrate each moment of joy and loving with thankfulness, and let the future take care of itself.

*The Durability of Jealousy.* Jealous behavior continues to be socially sanctioned in "appropriate" forms, but there are reasons to believe it will diminish as it ceases to serve a useful function in interpersonal relationships. Jessie Bernard believes: "If it is true that marriage is indeed moving away from the old monogamic format in the direction of some as yet unclarified form, jealousy in the classic form would no longer be required to support it and we could expect its gradual diminution. But until we know with more certainty the nature of the model—or models—of marriage we are moving toward, jealousy in some form or other may continue to crop up in the clinician's office."⁴ It is probable, also, that even as models of marriage are clarified and become culturally accepted, forms of jealousy will be experienced by most people to some degree some of the time. Whether one believes that jealousy is inevitable or eradicable, normal or neurotic, is ultimately not the most important issue. What is important is to ask the most helpful question: "What *kind* of jealousy affects my relationships?" It is of no practical use to try to decide once and for all whether or not one is a jealous person. But if one understands the various types of jealousy something *can* be done to control and minimize it—to disarm it if not dissolve it. Simply expressing jealousy is a copout in a relationship— it is not being honestly open to one's self or to the special other. So much more of the expectations and satisfactions of a relationship could be understood, communicated, and creatively acted upon, if couples could understand the specifics of jealousy. What is it that you *really* resent? Are you afraid? Envious? Excluded? Competitive? Possessive? Does your ego hurt? What do you *really* want to communicate to each other? It doesn't help merely to say "I'm jealous." Jealous how? Can we *do* something about it? Should we renegotiate our expectations of each other? How can we grow from here?

## JEALOUSY INVENTORY EXERCISE

A couple or a small group may gain insight into the specific meanings of jealous feelings by analyzing jealousy experiences according to the six types of jealousy described above.

A couple can simply write out or relate to each other their last remembered jealous experience and then try to rephrase the feelings more directly in terms of the six kinds of jealousy.

In a group of six or more, each person could write about a jealousy experience anonymously (without age, name, or sex). Shuffle papers and redistribute with each person reading the paper in hand and offering some possibilities for more direct expression of the experience: e.g., "this person felt left out"; "this person isn't aware of his/her partner's need for privacy"; "this person seems envious and unhappy about what he/she doesn't have"; etc.

If it doesn't feel right or comfortable to share a jealousy experience with a partner or a small group, use the following four examples for discussion. They were obtained in a small group and are shared as written. Were the writers male or female? How could they have expressed themselves directly and honestly to the person who occasioned the jealousy? What could each person *do* to improve the relationship or situation?

## Question: When was the last time you felt jealousy and how do you remember the experience?

*Example 1.* My last experience with jealousy took place when the person with whom I'm involved chose to spend a weekend vacationing without wanting to have me along. My feelings were very intense because for me there could be no real pleasure in a vacation without bringing this person. I was angry, hurt, rejected totally out of proportion to the occasion.

*Example 2.* I feel jealousy to *a limited* extent when my partner or I discover relations *as deep* as ours that were had before our present relationship.

I feel a *twinge* of jealousy when friends in a "family net-work" relationship have a tactile relationship with partner.

*Example 3.* Although I felt, and feel, that the sensual/sexual experience need not be confined exclusively to the mate or partner of the moment, I became extremely jealous, insecure, annihilated when this led to my partner's acute emotional involvement. By losing the partner's primary commitment to me, I was losing much of my identity.

*Example 4.* When I felt my mate was able to express feelings completely (not necessarily sexual) and I was not able to do so I felt jealous of this ability. This was not a threat on the part of my mate, but rather a feeling of a lacking on my part. My mate's warmth, concerns, fears, and hopes were able to be expressed and experienced but mine were hidden both to me and others.

# CHAPTER EIGHT / LIVING THE OPEN-ENDED MARRIAGE

O O O O O O O O O O O O O O O O O O O O O O O O O O
O O O O O O O O O O O O O O O O O O O O O O O O O O
O O O O O O O O O O O O O O O O O O O O O O O O O O
O O O O O O O O O O O O O O O O O O O O O O O O O O
O O O O O O O O O O O O O O O O O O O O O O O O O O
O O O O O O O O O O O O O O O O O O O O O O O O O O
O O O O O O O O O O O O O O O O O O O O O O O O O O
O O O O O O O O O O O O O O O O O O O O O O O O O O
O O O O O O O O O O O O O O O O O O O O O O O O O O

How sweet it would be if it could be said that the open-ended marriage has no problems. Alas, utopian monogamy is not available in a prescribed model of any kind. OEM certainly does have its problems, some of which are transitional due to entrenched attitudes against this alternative lifestyle. Since there is little knowledge and competence in dealing with OEM among professionals—even marriage counselors— there is no support system for this marital relationship; no moral support and no societal sanctions. This book, in fact, is written to change that abysmal situation. The questions people everywhere ask about OEM and their condemnation, interest, or anxiety, reveal much of what needs to be communicated about OEM. Public reaction also reveals the kinds of problems practitioners of OEM can anticipate. Quite naturally, OEM people will not all face the same difficulties since much depends on place of residence, financial status, type of occupation as well as the personality and character of the people involved. Some of the practical problems or difficult aspects of living an open-ended marriage will be listed and briefly discussed. No one couple will have them all, but to the extent that such problems can be openly discussed, guidelines will be developed for strong and joyful open-ended marriages. The listing is not in order of priority, but the first three of the fifteen problems are not inherent to OEM; they are caused by external factors. Equal attention will not be given to each of the problem areas.

## THE IMMORAL PUT-DOWN

It is almost impossible to get unsympathetic middle-aged professionals to accept emotionally the moral context of sex with someone in addition to a spouse. "Unfaithfulness," "adultery," and "promiscuity" inevitably become part of the accusatory question period. Because traditional morality focuses on the sex *act* so many people just cannot believe it is possible to be faithful to a *relationship* without being sexually exclusive. (See the discussion of adultery in chapter one.) Sexual experience with more than one person (spouse) is also labeled "promiscuous" with the emphasis again on the number of sexual partners rather than upon the quality of the relationships. Promiscuity relates to the abuse and misuse of relationships, not to the number of sexual partners. Younger people seem to understand contextual ethics more easily. And in some workshops and conferences responsiveness to alternative lifestyles coincides with a division of age groups; the younger people more open to new ideas (though not necessarily adopting them) and the older people more defensive about the traditional, inherited values (though not necessarily defending the status quo). The spiritual or religious values in open-ended marriage are much more easily perceived by youth, while older people tend to invoke the supposed sanctity of traditional monogamy. The irony is that the experiment in OEM is being led by progressive-minded middle-aged persons rather than by the "youth culture."

In any case, OEMers, whatever their age, should be prepared to be judged as immoral, blasphemous, and traitors to the one nation "under God."

## THE SICK PUT-DOWN

In contemporary society, the condemnation of the clergy-person is less feared than the judgment of the psychological counselor. It bothers few people to be told they are in danger of losing their souls, but some of those same people would take it on faith if they were told they were in danger of being emotionally sick. The righteous and dire warnings of an eminent marriage counselor are enough to make the jeremiads of the Puritan preacher Jonathan Edwards sound like Alka-Seltzer commercials.

"There are quite a few people of both sexes in our society," says Dr. Walter Stokes, "who make extramarital affairs a chronic and continuing pattern of life. Most of them do this because of neurotic disabilities which render them incapable of a loving, trusting, deeply satisfying sex relationship with anyone—in or out of marriage. These people spend their lives blindly groping about from one affair to the next, often creating severe problems for themselves and for others. The mate-swapping groups include many such persons. They are likely to be emotionally ill and require psychotherapeutic help if their neurotic handicaps are to be overcome."[1]

Dr. Stokes' categorical excommunication of a large number of people from the Church of Middle-Class White American Mental Health could be viewed as an interesting variety of secular religion were it not for the fact that it is accepted by the public as an *ex cathedra* proclamation from the Marriage Counseling Establishment. There are undoubtedly men and women who do go through life bouncing pin-ball fashion from one sexual episode to another. Such people are disturbed and directionless, *but not because they're having a variety of sex experiences*. At least they have occasional human contacts—contacts which bump them back into the game and keep them going. Dr. Stokes also believes that "When a venture outside marriage comes, it is usually entered into in a state of desperate frustration and marital misery. . . . Extramarital relations are rarely sought by spouses who are even moderately happy in their marriage."[2] In his effort to maintain the myth of Traditional-Marriage-as-Happiness, Dr. Stokes ignores the testimony of those who, for a variety of reasons, are convinced that extramarital sexual relationships have made them happier and have stabilized their marriage. There are thousands of sexually exclusive marriages in which both partners live lives of "quiet desperation."

Dr. Lonny Myers and the Rev. Hunter Leggitt have a more helpful approach to understanding extramarital sex than the sick put-down approach. They report:

" " " " "

We thought that people were driven to extramarital sex because either the marriage or the marriage partner was inadequate, but we discovered that it occurs whether the marriage is "good" or "bad." Often it fulfills needs which could not be fulfilled by any single relationship, within marriage or otherwise, no matter how "perfect."

We believed that a feeling of guilt is usually associated with extramarital sex. But we discovered that the persons we interviewed felt little or no guilt. And yet they were fully capable of experiencing guilt—for example, about striking a child, acting out of racial prejudice, and so on. Several stated, however, that they "would feel guilty" if, as a result of their extramarital sex lives, they neglected their families, became hostile to the sexual advances of their mates, or destroyed someone else's marriage. But they took unusual precautions to avoid these outcomes. In fact, most felt themselves to be "on the same team" with their lovers, with a real sense of respect for their obligations and marriages.[3]

" " " " "

Until greater numbers of people realize that there can be creative and moral uses of extramarital or comarital sex, OEMers should not be surprised when they meet others who assume that they are emotionally ill and require psychotherapeutic help.

## THE UNFIT EMPLOYEE PUT-DOWN

There are still authorities offering free cups of hemlock to undesirable corrupters of the youth and the state. The more usual method of disposal, however, is social ostracism and possible loss of job. In a democracy which cherishes and protects cultural pluralism, it is astonishing that there is yet no freedom for pluralism in sexual behavior, especially behavior which is private and among conscientious, mutually consenting persons. Fear shrouds the joy of many who are sexually unconventional; fear of creating S·C·A·N·D·A·L; fear of economic reprisals; fear of losing friends. Any professional or public-service employee can suffer financially for openly advocating alternative lifestyles, for the hypocrisy and intolerance of the defenders of public morality are vengeful. The absurd case of the minister who was fired by the elders for allowing his vivacious daughter to wear a bathing suit in a beauty contest is indicative of a pervasive prurient puritanism in this country.

It is time to resist the repression of the elders—and all who would make their own sex ethic the law—through legal reform, public education, and individual courage. The courage and action of Seth Many and Carolyn Peck, as revealed in their book *Lewd*, should be an inspiration to all who value sexual liberty and pluralism. Seth, trained as a psychiatrist, and Carolyn, trained as a lawyer, were both arrested for being nude in their own home. Members of the Cambridge Commune, which accepted nudity, Carolyn and Seth were observed working on their sunporch while naked. They brilliantly represented themselves at their trial, a trial which has implications for all who move beyond tradition. As Seth Many wrote: "The LEWD affair, in its modest origins was a prototypical confrontation of American liberal theory and Amerikan illiberal fact, a confrontation of religious and secular mythologies, a conflict of democratic vs. authoritarian traditions, a tediously personal yet profoundly universal recapitulation of the struggle of awareness for open expression."[4]

## SPECIAL AND PRIMARY RELATIONSHIPS

"When a husband and wife have built for themselves an open relationship based on equality, honest communication, and trust, when their liking for one another, their love and respect for one another is defined by mutual understanding rather than by predetermined role structures or the coercive clauses of the closed (marital) contract, then the bond they form between themselves will be the central focus of their lives. Their own marriage will be their primary relationship. Precisely because this bond is so deep, so secure and so central to their lives, they can afford to open it up and let others in."[5] The O'Neils rightly stress the centrality of the primary relationship in dyadic (two-people) marriage, the dynamic core for any marriage (including same-sex) with open-ended extensions.

However, it is one thing to believe that the responsibilities of the spouses to each other rank first in importance; it is another thing to experience *conflicts* in relational responsibilities. For there are times when one must risk conflict with the spouse in order to devote time and energy to another intimate relationship. The problems of jealousy and resentfulness because of felt neglect continue to arise and must be worked through patiently and gently. Sometimes it's hard to derive comfort from the reassurance that the relationship is *primary*; that's cold and impersonal sociological jargon. Something more emotionally powerful needs to be felt between the couple: an ongoing sense of specialness and common destiny; that sense of continuity of relationship and anticipation of future experiences which is unique in degree to marital intimacy. It's not so much a matter of being number one as it is a matter of feeling special while yet enjoying a number of other very special persons and relationships. *Every* close relationship is special in its own way and none of these relationships need threaten the special intimacy of marriage once the two partners *feel* secure in their trust in and desire for each other. Only loving, trusting behavior will create that reality, not elaborate contracts.

## THE TIMING OF EXTENSIONS

Ideally it would be delightful if couples could prepare each other for open-ended marriage *before* marriage. Certainly the qualities of healthy openness which the O'Neils describe should be tested out in the process of selecting a lover and life partner. The probability is, however, that the OEM model is a relationship that married couples will begin to work toward under various circumstances and with differing degrees of awareness. In many cases, it will not be until the first settlement phase of the marriage is lived—10 to 15 years—that one or both partners will desire the enrichment of open-ended relationships. There is no one blueprint for everyone to follow, but what needs to be realized is that significant personal growth and creative interpersonal relating will necessarily entail some anxiety and suffering. Risk-taking produces some anxiety, emotional growth requires painful self-criticism, and ventures in new relationships sometimes end in hurt or grief.

It is highly improbable that a couple will first reach an almost perfect relationship *before* they decide to open the relationship and let others in. It is more probable that the primary relationship will always be changing with some tension and unhappiness as well as with great joy and profound loving. Extended relationships may not be established at the most convenient time of the marriage and these problems will have to be worked through. There is something supercilious about people who maintain their moral superiority by granting to friends and lovers only the time "left over" in their marriage. There is basically no such thing as spare time in a marriage, especially when children are being nurtured, and sometimes friends and lovers require marital prime time. Also these co-marital relationships may supplement aspects of marriage rather than merely being something in addition to the marriage; they may be of substance, and not merely frosting on the cake.

## CHILDREN, PARENTS, AND STRAIGHT FRIENDS

Adults who are relatively secure in their chosen lifestyle have few hangups about their influence on their children. Believing in the rightness-for-them of their way of life, they are open with their children and unafraid of exposing them to new ideas and new relationships. Children, depending on their age, may become embarrassed or confused when they realize that their parents have other sexual friendships, but as in all other areas of education for human sexuality, forthright discussion and sharing of values at appropriate times is the best approach. What matters most as far as children are concerned, is the quality of relationship between parents, and if they are surrounded by other loving adults, so much the better. It is likely that children who share life with equalitarian and open parents will themselves develop in a self-actualizing manner and will be emotionally strong enough to determine their own lifestyles.

Grandparents and straight friends can be more of a problem than children. They ask embarrassing questions, for one thing. And they themselves are embarrassed when one of the spouses is seen in public with an extramarital friend. Strange, by the way, that they should be embarrassed only when the extramarital friend is of the other sex!

The term "straight" can, unfortunately, be used in a disparaging and judgmental manner, and such usage should be discouraged. It is here used as shorthand to refer to people who hold conventional sexual and marital values: exclusively heterosexual and sexually exclusive. Straight friends who remain friends are a great joy, for their friendship is based on acceptance of other persons in terms of who they are rather than in terms of social conformity.

## ONE-HALF OEM

It is possible to find an open-ended marriage with only one open-ended spouse. We are not referring here to the usual double-standard, hypocritical extramarital affair. *Both* partners share the values of sexual/sensual openness, but one partner may choose not to actualize this freedom. This situation can produce some difficulties such as assumptions of others that the nonparticipating partner is sexually inadequate or cold. Usually, direct communication can clear up any misunderstandings.

What is much more difficult is the situation where partners discover that their sexual values are vastly different and that one wants to move toward OEM while the other wants to maintain a sexually exclusive relationship. This can be an extremely painful situation which may or may not be resolved through marriage counseling—if one partner will not compromise constructively, the counseling may make clear the unpromising aspects of the relationship and lead to greater unhappiness if not separation/divorce. Most therapists and counselors would reinforce the values of the partner with traditional values and try to "cure" the other partner while "enriching" the marriage. Which partner—if either—should compromise depends on their total relationship and their priority of shared values.

## DISBELIEVERS AND CASUAL SEX

There is a general problem category which has to do with the disbelief, anxiety, or fear of potential sexual/sensual friends.

While some manipulators may try to con others into sex episodes by pretending to have an open-ended marriage, there is an uneasiness toward all OEMers, especially on the part of single adults. The suspicion or uneasiness can, of course, be justifiable—it is better to be cautious than to be exploited. Because OEM openly practiced is so relatively new a lifestyle, OEMers will be dismissed by some as dirty old men/women; there will be anxiety over the anticipated reaction of the spouse ("What if your wife/husband finds out?"); and there will be guilt feelings over casual sex experience.

The responsibility hangup causes tremendous confusion. It is a more sophisticated version of "It's okay as long as you really love me." Not all experiences of mutual sensual pleasuring will be based on deep, continued commitments which are supposed to be more "responsible." Actually, even casual or one-time experiences demand as much sensitivity and responsiveness as more serious commitments. The fullness of integrity and caring ought to be brought to every human encounter, and a casual sex experience is a capsulized reflection of one's personality and character. Sex and/or sensual pleasuring between two people who have known each other for only one day can be a magnificently human way of saying thank you and good-bye; a way of communicating, "I appreciate you and enjoyed being with you." It is important to emphasize that sensual pleasuring doesn't necessarily involve intercourse.

## PROBLEM RELATIONSHIPS

It should be obvious that not all co-marital episodes are positive experiences. There is a wide range of negative happenings which are risked, especially in the initial ventures. Some possibilities:

unexpected sado-masochism;

possessiveness and persistent telephone calls;

a lover who becomes too serious in the sense of expecting marriage;

loud-mouths who simply like to collect people and then gossip;

unrealistic expectations of sexual performance;

friends/lovers who become emotionally dependent.

Through experience and disciplined selectivity one can learn to avoid relationships with a high risk of negative impact and to invest one's self in friendships which will be more mutually rewarding than troublesome.

## *MONEY, OR WHO SPENT THE LAST BUCK?*

Except for the fortunate minority of wealthy people, everybody else has financial problems which severely limit options for fun and vacations. The problem is so obvious and common that it requires little discussion here, the major point being the importance of spouses openly discussing it with each other—and with their other lovers. Especially in a situation where only one spouse has an income, there is a tendency to limit more severely the financial freedom of the partner. The entertainment and recreation needs of the married couple merit primary attention in order for there to be fun and enriching experiences in their shared lives. And then the matter of how much nonfamily spending money each is periodically allotted should be mutually agreed upon. Whatever arrangements are devised, the important thing is that each spouse feel fairly treated as far as money is concerned.

Finances may also be an appropriate matter for discussion with extramarital friends, since one should not pridefully expend more money than he/she can really afford.

## *VD AND PREGNANCY—THE OLD THREATS*

There is no sense at all in avoiding these unpleasant issues, for only by being alert to their threats can we defend against them. VD is rampant on a worldwide scale, and the rate of contagion will likely continue to increase until vaccines are developed. The trouble with gonorrhea, for example, is that it

is not easily detected in women, although there are encouraging developments toward the solution of this problem. It
can also be asymptomatic in men. In the meantime, however,
it would be well for women to request testing for gonorrhea
as regularly and as casually as they have the pap smear test.
Venereal disease only becomes a moral problem when it is
willfully passed on to someone else, otherwise it is simply a
matter of medical treatment and should be no more embarrassing than seeking help for an ear infection.
Unplanned pregnancies create nothing but misery, and
unwanted babies can be a menace to the human race. While an
early abortion may be the best solution to an extramarital
pregnancy, the problem should not be allowed to occur in the
first place. If the pill is not used, a combination of other contraceptives should be used to insure against any one contraceptive
failure. For couples who already have children serious consideration should be given to surgical procedures for producing
sterility—for example, vasectomy or laparoscopy. In an open-
ended marriage, it is not enough for the husband to have a
vasectomy since the wife would have to stay on the pill or
use other contraceptive means (unless, of course, she chooses
only vasectomized males!). Until the day when oral or
injected contraceptives are available for males, heterosexual
lovers will continue to put the burden of highly effective contraception on the female. Whatever decisions couples may
make concerning preferred and medically safe contraception,
the subject should be seriously discussed, and if no contraception is employed, intercourse should be avoided. There are
other ways of sensual pleasuring which can be enjoyed without
the awesome risk of pregnancy. And if there is contraceptive
failure and pregnancy occurs, abortion, if chosen, should be
undertaken as early as possible. One of the purposes of extended intimate relationships is to produce pleasure and joy,
not babies and misery.

It sounds patronizing to talk to adults in simplistic terms
about VD prevention and absolute contraceptive protection,
but sex counselors are painfully aware of the tragedy which
can result from benign neglect of these serious issues.

## IDENTIFYING WITH THE LOVER'S LOVER

One of the distinguishing characteristics of open-ended marriage is the optional privacy of co-marital relationships—spouses don't have to know each other's lovers and intimate friends. There is, however, an ethical dimension not only to the awareness of the primary relationship of one's intimate married friends but to the actual personhood of a lover's spouse. In the framework of a heterosexual extramarital relationship, the ethical dimension is felt in terms of identifying with members of one's own sex; to one's brothers or sisters. Both the Women's Liberation and Gay Liberation movements have increased our awareness of how we mistreat members of the same sex: women have been women's most intimate enemy, and men have supported the sexist privileges of each other, but have been unable to be emotionally close to each other. How, then, do we relate to our unknown sisters or brothers who are primary lovers to our lovers? Even though we may not know them personally, how can we allow them to be hurt or degraded in any way? This issue is fantastically intriguing and complex—it merits a book of its own, as do several of the problem areas in open-ended marriage.

One practical problem, for example, is the extent to which one should challenge the sexist-awareness-level of one's co-marital lover. Men, for instance, often complain about their ʿwives—to what extent should a female lover defend her lover's wife? Probably to the utmost. When one woman is condemned all women are condemned, and how can any liberated woman be emotionally or sexually responsive to a man who demeans his wife? Double-standard men are so incredibly stupid. Case in point:

" " " " "

After a luxuriously expensive evening on the town, Marsha and Ted went to a plush hotel suite to enjoy each other physically. Marsha, an intelligent, married, liberated woman had been meeting Ted over the past year—each time he came into town on a business venture. It was a passionate relationship and each of them eagerly anticipated their times together. During the course of this particular evening, while Marsha and Ted were caressing each other and simultaneously sharing their thoughts, Ted blurted out, "If my wife ever let another man touch her, I'd kill the whore." Ted could never understand why Marsha would never see him again.

" " " " "

Time and time again, women are turned off by men who unconsciously reveal their double standard, their disdain for their wives, or their ignorant pride in female conquest.

Men, also, have similar experiences of discovering that their female lovers scorn their husbands without being knowledgeable or sensitive to their husband's or male lover's legitimate needs.

## SHARING LOVING FRIENDS

Perhaps the ultimate test of trust and openness in an open-ended marriage is the ability of spouses to share with each other their most valued friends. This sharing is not a precondition of OEM—it is something that usually develops spontaneously, and it can be a very awkward process. When the intimate friend of a wife (male or female) becomes intimate with the husband (or vice versa) there is often a period of silent testing to determine trust levels. The third-person friend has the most difficult situation in that loyalty to each may be in conflict with loyalty to both.

There is tremendous value in having same-sex intimate friends (no genital sex involved necessarily) with whom one can simply dump one's problems and fears. When that same friend becomes intimate with one's spouse/lover there is the anxiety of loss and the threat of betrayal. It takes persons with a high degree of self-esteem to allow with gladness the sharing of loving friends.

## TIME FOR INTIMACY

Partners in a creative marriage can hardly find enough time for each other (and any children), especially if both have professional careers or jobs in addition to the work of home maintenance, interpersonal care, and child nurture. Time for extramarital relationships must be planned deliberately. This does not rule out spontaneity by any means, but even the freedom for spontaneity is an accomplishment, for it depends on the understanding and cooperation of OEM partners. Lack of sustained time together on the part of extramarital lovers is agonizingly frustrating. Always so much has to be condensed into so little time. Even when an entire twenty-four hours can be spent together once a month, there is just not enough time to bring each other up to date and express the fullness and intensity of one's feelings. Neither the utopianism of Robert Rimmer's "synergamous marriage" or the leisure of the four-day work week will solve this exquisite dilemma.

## SEPARATION GRIEF AND RESOLUTION

We have no guidelines for separation grief in our culture. We not only deny physical death through our lugubrious synonyms for mortality; we also pretend that all loving relationships are meant to last forever. We simply do not know how to let each other go. When we experience a joyful episode with someone we tend to want to repeat it. But instead of appreciating the reality of a celebrative experience we can deaden it by idolizing it in sentimental memorials. There does not exist a relational ethic which prepares us to cope for the ending of sublime relationships. We are either supposed to keep them or fail in them, and neither of those extreme options describes where we live and move and have our being. The absurdity of all or nothing relationships distorts the wondrous range of our relational capabilities. There is so much that we can learn from the married clients who gave a gift to their counselor on their last session. It was a quotation from the ancient stoic Seneca: "To lose a friend is the greatest of all evils, but endeavor rather to rejoice that you possessed him than to mourn his loss." Celebrate the joy of friendship while it lives, and when people or circumstances change, continue to rejoice in the blessings of affection rather than curse the pain of loss.

## BEYOND THE PROBLEMS

Persons who support each other in open-ended marriage live in amazing grace. All relationships involve risk-taking, problems, and crises, but there is a choice in the quality and meaning of such dilemmas—we needn't be passive victims of human folly and mystery. Open-ended marriage is not, by definition, any "better" than any other alternative lifestyle, but for those who choose it there is a continual sense of joyful value-venturing. Problems become background to self-actualization in the context of shared humanistic tenderness and empathy. The spectrum of intimate friendship is always open, and the opportunities for human contact with affection are never arbitrarily closed. There is not much of lasting substance to base one's being upon except the realization of warmth, joy, and support in relationships. And when that essential dimension of living is absent, all social causes are hollow. Humankind does not live by ideology alone—when intimacy with others is denied, involvement in social reformation is more revenge than affirmation and celebration.

What the model of open-ended marriage offers is the possibility of a vibrant monogamy which embraces the being of any other person who seeks the grace of human caring and touch.

# NOTES

## CHAPTER ONE

### OPEN-ENDED MARRIAGE VERSUS ADULTERY

1. Ronald Mazur, "Beyond Morality: Toward the Humanization of the Sexes," presented at the National Council on Family Relations, Chicago, October 1970. Also published in *Forum* magazine (London, June 1971).
2. Paul Gebhard, quoted by Morton Hunt in *The Affair* (World Publishing Co., 1969), p. 11.
3. Ben B. Lindsey with Wainwright Evans, *The Companionate Marriage* (Boni and Liveright, 1927), p. v.
4. Arthur H. Hirch, *The Love Elite* (Julian Press, Inc., 1963).
5. *Towards a Quaker View of Sex*, an essay by a group of Friends (Friends Home Service Committee, London, 1964).
6. John F. Cuber and Peggy B. Harroff, *The Significant Americans* (Appleton-Century, 1965).
7. Rustum and Della Roy, *Honest Sex* (The New American Library, 1968).
8. Joyce Peterson and Marilyn Mercer, *Adultery for Adults* (Coward-McCann, 1968).
9. Morton Hunt, *The Affair* (World Publishing Co., 1969).
10. Gerhard Neubeck, ed., *Extramarital Relations* (Prentice-Hall, Inc., 1969).
11. Eugene Scheimann, "A New Kind of Adultery," *Sexology* (February 1971).
12. Jack Valenti speaking of the film "Ryan's Daughter," quoted in *Time* (May 31, 1971).

## CHAPTER TWO

### THE DOUBLE STANDARD AND PEOPLE'S LIBERATION

1. Ira L. Reiss, "Premarital Sexual Standards" in *Sexuality and Man*, edited by SIECUS (Charles Scribner and Sons, 1970), p. 40.
2. Shulamith Firestone, *The Dialectic of Sex* (William Morrow and Co., 1970), pp. 160–161.

3. See Ronald Mazur, *Commonsense Sex* (Beacon Press, 1968), pp. 31–34.

4. Jessie Bernard, "Women, Marriage, and the Future," *The Futurist* (April 1970), pp. 41–43.

5. Albert Ellis and Albert Abarbanal, eds., *The Encyclopedia of Sexual Behavior* (Hawthorn Books, 1961).

6. Alice S. Rossi, "Equality Between the Sexes: An Immodest Proposal," *Daedalus* (Spring, 1964), p. 608.

7. John H. Gagnon and William Simon, "Prospects for Change in American Sexual Patterns," *Medical Aspects of Human Sexuality* (January 1970), p. 113.

8. David Reuben, *Everything You Always Wanted to Know About Sex But Were Afraid to Ask* (David McKay Co., 1969), pp. 129–151.

9. Arnold Birenbaum, "Revolution Without the Revolution: Sex in Contemporary America," *The Journal of Sex Research* (November 1970), p. 266.

## CHAPTER THREE

### NEEDED: NEW ATTITUDES TOWARD INTIMACY

1. Mary Breasted, *Oh, Sex Education* (Praeger Publishers, 1970).

2. For example, Arnold Silverman, "Learn About Sex, Or Else," *Forum* (American edition, August 1972), pp. 12–15.

3. See Edward Sagarin, *The Anatomy of Dirty Words* (Lyle Stuart, 1962); see also *ETC* magazine, special issue on "Semantics and Sexuality" (June 1968).

## CHAPTER FOUR

### INTIMACY AND SENSUAL RESPONSIVENESS

1. a. "*J*," *The Sensuous Woman* (Lyle Stuart, 1969).
   b. "*M*," *The Sensuous Man* (Lyle Stuart, 1971).
   c. "*Mr. and Mrs. K*," *The Couple* (Berkley Publishing Corp., 1971).
   d. David Reuben, *Any Woman Can* (David McKay Co., Inc., 1971).

2. Ashley Montagu, *Touching: The Human Significance of Skin* (Columbia University Press, 1971), p. 167.

3. John Money, *Sex Errors of the Body* (Johns Hopkins Press, 1968).

4. William H. Masters and Virginia E. Johnson, *Human Sexual Inadequacy* (Little, Brown and Co., 1970), p. 10.

## CHAPTER FIVE

### VARIETIES OF ALTERNATIVE LIFESTYLES AND MODES OF SEXUAL BEHAVIOR

1. Larry L. Constantine and Joan M. Constantine, *Group Marriage: A Study of Contemporary Multilateral Marriage* (Macmillan, 1973). Also contains a bibliography of their many articles.
2. Robert Rimmer, *Thursday, My Love* (New American Library, 1972). It was the second of Bob Rimmer's seven previous books (*The Harrad Experiment*, 1966), which established him as the foremost American architect of sexual liberation within the context of the human potential movement.

## CHAPTER SIX

### DIVORCE AND THE OPEN-ENDED MARRIAGE

1. Elizabeth Janeway, *Man's World—Woman's Place: A Study in Social Mythology* (William Morrow and Co., Inc., 1971), pp. 221–222.
2. See Richard Farson, "Why Good Marriages Fail," *McCall's* (October 1971).
3. Abraham Maslow, *Motivation and Personality* (Harper and Brothers, 1954), p. 213.
4. For example: "If the marital maladjustment cannot be remedied with the aid of counseling, it is wiser to obtain a divorce before either party seeks another liaison." Robert A. Harper and Walter Stokes, *45 Levels to Sexual Understanding and Enjoyment* (Prentice-Hall, 1971), p. 149.

## CHAPTER SEVEN

### BEYOND JEALOUSY AND POSSESSIVENESS

1. David Mace, *Success in Marriage* (Abington Press, 1958), p. 11.
2. Nena and George O'Neil, *Open Marriage* (M. Evans Inc., 1972), p. 246.
3. Jessie Bernard, "Jealousy in Marriage," *Medical Aspects of Human Sexuality* (April 1971), p. 209.
4. *Ibid.*

CHAPTER EIGHT

LIVING THE OPEN-ENDED MARRIAGE

1. Robert A. Harper and Walter Stokes, *45 Levels to Sexual Understanding and Enjoyment* (Prentice-Hall, 1971), p. 149.

2. Walter Stokes, *ibid.*, p. 147.

3. Lonny Myers and Hunter Leggitt, "A New View of Adultery," *Sexual Behavior* (February 1972).

4. Seth Many and Carolyn Peck, *Lewd: The Inquisition of Seth and Carolyn* (Beacon Press, 1972), p. 1.

5. Nena and George O'Neil, *Open Marriage* (M. Evans, Inc., 1972), pp. 176–177.

# INDEX